Dec. 2010

Enjoy Food Memories of L'Aquila

LOVE,
Roberto & Marcia

BREAKING BREAD IN *L'Aquila*

BREAKING BREAD IN *L'Aquila*

Maria Filice

**FFP**

FOOD & FATE
PUBLISHING
*New York*

Copyright © 2010 Maria Filice.

All rights reserved. No portion of this book may be reproduced or transmitted in any form by any means, electronic, mechanical, photocopying, recording, or otherwise, without permission in writing from the publisher. For information on getting permission for reprints or excerpts, contact foodandfate@telospress.com.

Published in the United States by Food & Fate Publishing, an imprint of Telos Press Publishing.

Printed in the United States of America
15 14 13 12 11 10    1 2 3 4 5

ISBN 978-0-914386-43-8

Library of Congress Cataloging-in-Publication Data

Filice, Maria.
 Breaking bread in L'Aquila / by Maria Filice.
     p. cm.
 ISBN 978-0-914386-43-8
1.  Cookery, Italian. 2.  Cookery—Italy—L'Aquila.  I. Title.
 TX723.F545 2010
 641.5945—dc22
                                2009053960


Food & Fate Publishing
An Imprint of Telos Press Publishing
431 East 12th Street
New York, NY 10009

www.telospress.com/foodandfate

To my late husband, Paul Piccone

# Table of Contents

Introduction  9

Acknowledgements  11

How to use *Breaking Bread in L'Aquila*  13

My Entertaining Philosophy  15

Wines of Abruzzo  17

Trattoria San Biagio  20

## MONDAY

***Antipasti*** Bruschetta  24
***Primi Piatti*** Pasta e Fagioli (Pasta and Beans)  26
***Primi Piatti*** Pasta con Salsa di Maiale (Pasta with a Pork Tomato Sauce)  28
***Secondi Piatti*** Cotolette di Vitello (Veal Cutlets)  30
***Contorni*** Insalata con Scaglie di Parmigiano (Romaine Lettuce Salad with Shaved Parmigiano Cheese)  32
***Contorni*** Verdure Rustiche con Riduzione di Aceto Balsamico (Rustic Vegetables with Balsamic Reduction)  34
***Dolci*** Biscotti Amaretti (Amaretti Cookies)  36

## TUESDAY

***Antipasti*** Prosciutto e Melone (Prosciutto with Melon)  40
***Primi Piatti*** Minestra di Farro (Spelt Soup)  42
***Primi Piatti*** Spaghetti al Pomodoro (Spaghetti with Tomato Sauce)  44
***Secondi Piatti*** Baccalà al Forno (Baked Salt Cod)  46
***Secondi Piatti*** Peperoni Arrostiti Ripieni con Salsiccia (Roasted Stuffed Peppers with Sausage)  48
***Contorni*** Rapini (Broccoli Rabe)  50
***Dolci*** Crostata d'Albicocca (Rustic Apricot Fruit Tart)  52

## WEDNESDAY

***Antipasti*** Insalata Caprese (Caprese Salad)  56
***Primi Piatti*** Minestra di Verdure con Riso (Vegetable Soup with Rice)  58
***Primi Piatti*** Pasta al Forno con Pomodori e Capperi (Baked Pasta with Tomatoes and Capers)  60
***Secondi Piatti*** Costolette d'Agnello alla Griglia (Grilled Lamb Chops)  62
***Contorni*** Carciofi al Forno (Baked Artichokes)  64
***Contorni*** Patate Lesse con Prezzemolo Fresco (Boiled Potatoes with Fresh Parsley)  66
***Dolci*** Torta di Mele (Apple Cake)  68

## THURSDAY

***Antipasti*** Melanzane alla Griglia con Olive e Basilico (Grilled Eggplant with Cured Black Olives and Basil) 72

***Primi Piatti*** Gnocchi al Sugo di Pomodoro (Gnocchi with Tomato Sauce) 74

***Primi Piatti*** Pasta con Funghi (Pasta with Mushrooms) 76

***Secondi Piatti*** Maiale all'Arancia (Orange Glazed Pork) 78

***Secondi Piatti*** Scaloppine al Vino Bianco (Veal Scaloppine in White Wine) 80

***Contorni*** Finocchio e Cipolle Caramellizate con Scorza d'Arancia (Caramelized Fennel and Onions with Orange Rind) 82

***Dolci*** Biscotti 84

## FRIDAY

***Antipasti*** Insalata di Mare e Servita nel Radicchio (Seafood Salad in a Radicchio Cup) 88

***Primi Piatti*** Pasta con Salsa di Mascarpone e Zafferano (Pasta with a Saffron Mascarpone Sauce) 90

***Secondi Piatti*** Dentice al Forno con Salsa di Burro e Limone (Baked Red Snapper with a Lemon-Butter Sauce) 92

***Contorni*** Fagiolini all'Agro (Green Beans with Lemon) 94

***Contorni*** Fritto Misto di Funghi (Sautéed Mushrooms Medley) 96

***Contorni*** Peperoni Arrostiti (Roasted Peppers) 98

***Dolci*** Torta di Caffè (Coffee Cake) 100

## SATURDAY

***Antipasti*** Panini Imbottiti (Panini Appetizer) 104

***Primi Piatti*** Pasta e Lenticchie (Pasta and Lentils) 106

***Primi Piatti*** Spaghetti Aglio, Olio, e Peperoncino (Spaghetti with Garlic, Oil, and Chili Peppers) 108

***Secondi Piatti*** Pollo Arrosto con Aglio e Rosmarino (Roasted Chicken with Rosemary and Garlic) 110

***Contorni*** Cavolfiori al Forno (Baked Cauliflower) 112

***Contorni*** Piselli e Guanciale (Peas and Guanciale) 114

***Dolci*** Torta di Noci (Walnut Cake) 116

## SUNDAY

***Antipasti*** Crostini 120

***Primi Piatti*** Pasta alla Chitarra con Polpettine di Paolo (Pasta alla Chitarra with Paul's Meatballs) 122

***Primi Piatti*** Le Lasagne di Paolo (Paul's Lasagna) 124

***Secondi Piatti*** Cosciotto d'Agnello Arrosto (Roast Leg of Lamb) 126

***Contorni*** Patate Arrostite (Oven-Roasted Potatoes) 128

***Contorni*** Insalata di Rucola e Radicchio (Arugula and Radicchio Salad) 130

***Dolci*** Pizzelle 132

Pantry Page 134

Measurement Conversions 136

Index 138

# Introduction

The sun glitters through the rows of chestnut trees that lead to my favorite piazza in L'Aquila. An old friend and I sit eating our *crocante*, perfectly toasted panini sandwiches of mozzarella, prosciutto, and sweet ripe tomatoes. This—and a glass of one of Abruzzo's wonderful red wines—makes me very happy. It's fall, and we can hear the tap of the chestnuts as they hit the ground. We laugh and hope that we won't be the target of one of these hard and shiny chocolate-colored fruits. We forget, for just a moment, that this once vibrant and vivacious city is now saddened by the loss of so many residents, and many more homes and businesses in the devastating April 2009 earthquake. I've come back now to visit the town that held so many memories and to look for the people and flavors that I found here so many times, over many years

*Breaking Bread in L'Aquila* is not only a collection of fabulous recipes inspired by my visits to this beautiful Italian city, but it also represents a bittersweet, nostalgic journey. My late husband, Paul Piccone, was born in gorgeous L'Aquila. Thanks to him, I had the opportunity to visit and break bread on many occasions in this and many other towns in his homeland. Paul passed away five years ago, and he was spared the sadness of seeing his beloved native city devastated by the fateful force of nature.

But this is not a sad story. This is, in fact, a celebration of life and love—and, of course, food! With this book, I honor the memory of my late husband, the residents of L'Aquila and nearby towns who perished in the earthquake, and the scores of survivors who continue to speak lovingly of their home, though currently they are unable to inhabit it as before. Italy, a country far away from my home in New York, is a place I've always felt attached to—even before I married Paul. Though I was born and raised in Toronto, Canada, my parents came from Cosenza, Calabria. Despite the chilly winters in my parents' new home across the ocean, the influence of the old country—the way we spoke, lived, and ate—was always present.

Although many people, especially older aunts and grandparents, swore I was someone "who could never be tamed by a man," it was not so surprising to them that I ended up marrying an Italian who had moved from Abruzzo to New York. When I met Paul in 1990, I quickly became enamored of his brilliance, sense of humor, love of food—and the feeling I had grown up with, the desire to break bread with those whose company I enjoyed.

Paul was proud to bring me back to the land of his birth, and we had the opportunity to travel to Abruzzo on numerous occasions. Each time we would visit his favorite trattoria, San Biagio, which was conveniently located off of one of L'Aquila's beautiful piazzas, near a couple of the ninety-nine churches that adorn Paul's home city. We would visit Luciano and Andrea, the brother restaurateurs, and enjoy their company and home-cooked fare. Visiting was akin to going to a relative's home for dinner: we felt cozy, warm, and always well fed.

This welcoming tradition was something we also brought to our own *casa*, our home in the East Village of New York City. Almost immediately after we married in 1997, I had the honor to begin meeting more of Paul's friends and colleagues associated with the journal he had founded, *Telos*. Paul was a larger than life person, who created a lively intellectual circle sustained by his distinctive style of breaking bread by hosting legendary dinners, with delicious food and often very heated debates. Our apartment became a center for food and philosophy! Today I am happy to be able to continue this important tradition at the annual *Telos* conferences.

At first, Paul was the chef, and having grown up in a home where women dominated the cooking scene, I was totally smitten by his cooking prowess. But soon he let me into the kitchen (I was the first and only woman allowed there!), and he fueled me with constant accolades. Inspired by the food of my youth, our frequent visits to Italy, as well as Paul's favorite menu items, I was so happy to spend time in the kitchen creating—and recreating—many, many meals. Because of this, there was never a dull moment in our dining room! During our seven-and-a-half-year marriage, which sadly ended when Paul lost his battle with cancer, we enjoyed nightly dinners together, in the United States and Europe, mostly with guests, who joined us in relishing both company and food.

This book is a collection of some of my favorite dishes. Primarily from the L'Aquila region of Abruzzo, these easily accessible, fast (I've been doing 30-minute meals for years!), and tasty dishes are guaranteed to make you, your family, and your friends very happy. Through *Breaking Bread in L'Aquila*, I hope you'll join me in recognizing and appreciating these fabulous flavors. Perhaps you'll discover new taste combinations, or rediscover ones from your own heritage. The idea is to take this delicious journey and to enjoy every moment of it!

Alla salute! To your health! .

Maria Filice

# Acknowledgements

While I sat listening to Paul's peers and *Telos* editors speak at his memorial, I was moved by their words and how they described Paul as their mentor and number-one teacher. All said they had become better writers, editors, professors, and cooks. I feel blessed for the years that I knew Paul, and I am honored to dedicate my first book to him. As I worked on the book, Paul's voice echoed, and at times I could hear him edit my recipes with "what about *pasta alla chittara*" or his famous "*lasagne*." My conversation with him over the last five years has helped me to understand him in ways that put closure on things, and now I am about to begin a new chapter. I am certain that he is very proud.

To my mother, Amelia, a woman whom I have admired for her positive outlook on life. I don't think I've ever heard her speak negatively about anyone. A saint perhaps? To my *nonna* Chiarina, who was tough and possessed a sharp wit, yet still remained very feminine—a woman who learned to mask pain through her humor. Not a saint but a remarkable woman.

To my father, Peter, who continues to be a big part of my life and still considers me his little girl.

To Frank, my younger brother who along with me, was referred to as "*mezza capo*" by our father. Our sharing the same temperment made me strong-willed as the only girl. Thank you for your great sense of humor. You always know what to say to put a smile on my face!

To John, my best friend. Your intuitive positive energy is a gift. Thank you for always being my big brother.

To my sisters-in-law, Daniela and Maria, thank you for translating and testing recipes and thanks for being part of my family.

To my nieces and nephews, Peter, Alessandra, Larissa, Vanessa, Amelia, and Stefano, you give me unconditional love and inspire my playful inner child.

To my cousin, Anna, who has shared so many memories and who is the sister that I never had. You bring music and dance into my kitchen.

To my cousin, Renée Angela Filice, thanks for always nudging me about writing. I will treasure our L'Aquila trip and your beautiful watercolor painting of San Biagio.

To Frances Maone, thanks for helping me get through the toughest period of my life. Without you, I don't think that I could have finished this book on time. Thank you for your invaluable "no measuring friendship."

Thanks to Jocelyn Klemm for your expertise with the wine section and for helping me to realize my dream. I also want to thank Ric Kitowski (her spouse) for his advice and support. I'm so lucky to have you guys in my kitchen!

To Christina, my close friend. I know Paul would be very pleased that I chose you as my confidante. I'm so lucky to have you and Juan in my life. You truly have made my life in New York so much richer!

To Andrea and Luciano Di Carlofelice, owners of San Biagio, a place that Paul and I enjoyed visiting many times. It was during a visit in October 2004 that I was inspired to fulfill my lifelong dream to write a book. At the time, I wondered if the cookbook was my way of dealing with my grief, but I also knew that there was magic in the idea. I want to thank Andrea and Luciano for sharing some favorite recipes. The brothers inspired me to recreate tastes in my own versions and words.

To Elena Aga-Rossi, thank you for introducing me to Anna Maria Iorio from the University of L'Aquila. Anna Maria introduced me to one of her students, Alessandra Circo, who was instrumental with transcribing the recipes in Italian. She and I have formed a bond like sisters.

To Arlen Gagliano, for helping me to put my first book together, thanks for our memorable trip to L'Aquila. I dedicate the panini recipe to you, and I will cherish our daily walks and talks to our favorite panini bar!

I want to thank Russell Berman who supported my decision to continue publishing *Telos* and who is now my editor, close friend, and mentor—indeed a home run!

To Brendan Bathrick, Art Director. Thanks for understanding my vision.

To Robert Richardson, *Telos* Managing Editor. Thanks for helping me to execute my vision.

To Carolyn Pulford, my photographer. Thank you for introducing yourself at "Rick's" and for photographing my dishes through my eyes.

To Corrado Paina, thank you for inspiring me to come up with the title *Breaking Bread in L'Aquila*, a title that speaks more than words.

To the following people who have contributed to and supported my project: Marilena Filice, David Pan, Nathalie Murray, Allie Simmons, James Miner, Barbara Bauer, Sara Spinelli, David Nudo, Joe Angellotti, Darcie Rowan, Meg McAllister, Jennifer Almouli, Diana McKendree, and the extended community of Telos Press.

# How to use Breaking Bread in L'Aquila

Italians, in my experience, are unlike Canadians and Americans in the way they eat, prepare, and enjoy food. In my house, even as we were eating one meal, we'd be talking about the next one. Though I didn't realize it as a child (it was just the way we did it!), I now know that our style was quite different from that of my peers.

For many years now, my friends have been telling me that I should collect my recipes (many spontaneously inspired, thanks to what looked good at the market, what was on sale, or what I had in my pantry) and share them with the world. It's funny: although I used to make fun of my mother, grandmother, and aunts due to their inability to "clearly" dictate a recipe to me ("Maria, you just put a bit of this with a little of that and that's how you make it!"), I found myself following their kitchen rules of doing things by touch and taste instead of by measurements. (Could it be in my DNA?) But here, in *Breaking Bread in L'Aquila*, I've finally written down the amounts, yields, and procedures, in a way that is accessible to everyone.

The idea of this book is to give you a wealth of serving and cooking options. The recipes are organized according to the days of the week, and for each day there are the following choices:

1) ***Antipasti***: These are usually enjoyed before a meal, but you can also make them as a meal or main course, perhaps with a salad and a nice glass of wine.

2) ***Primi Piatti***: These "First Course" dishes are typically our pasta dishes, usually served before the main dish. Again, these are also perfect as a main dish.

3) ***Secondi Piatti***: This collection of "Second Course" dishes could be described as main dishes. This is usually the course in which meat or fish is served.

4) ***Contorni***: These are side dishes, typically served along with a main dish, but also versatile and hearty enough to be expanded and served as a meal.

5) ***Dolci***: These are desserts, which are perfect for after lunch, dinner, or perhaps afternoon tea, coffee, or even breakfast.

For each day, the dishes presented are designed to complement each other. Also, each recipe contains an introduction in which there are serving suggestions and modifications. I don't think you'll make all of each day's selections on one day, though you might if you were making a buffet dinner for a crowd.

Speaking of serving dinner for a crowd, I'm also including something that I always enjoy: some suggested wines to accompany these dishes. All are from the Abruzzo region. This overview is meant to serve as a guide, not a must-have list.

Don't worry about following the days of the week. If you want to prepare Monday's recipes on Thursday, then go ahead—there are no rules! What I suggest is that you first look through the table of contents to check them all out. Then, go back and see which dishes you'd like to try together. After that, it's time to start cooking!

Don't be afraid to use these recipes as guidelines, and to vary them according to what you and your family and friends enjoy. For example, while there are many meat dishes, I also include plenty of vegetarian fare—and, as you'll see, you can follow my tips and easily adapt the dishes in whichever way you like. Actually, my only rules would be that you use ingredients that are fresh, local, and natural, and that you serve them in big, practical plates. As you can see from my photos, which were all taken with my dishes and in my home, I enjoy setting up my dinners in a particular way. But this is just my way. You should find out what works best for you, and take it from there!

# My Entertaining Philosophy

It's not all about the flowers, not all about the table, not even all about the food. (Okay, it is a lot about the food!) But really, my entertaining philosophy is simple: it's all about creating a warm, personal, and welcoming atmosphere. Here are my six golden rules for entertaining:

### 1. Know your guests

Make sure you ask, prior to menu planning, what your guests' allergies or dietary restrictions are (include drinking preferences and restrictions) and what they like and dislike. This sets a warm tone and conveys the message that you are interested in making each of your guests feel special.

### 2. Find the right wine

Remember that the most important consideration is that your guests enjoy it. Use the suggestions on pages 18–19 as a guide to help you choose from the Abruzzo region.

### 3. Let your guests serve themselves

I've always been a big fan of family-style eating. Having people help themselves (and encouraging them to go back for seconds) makes people feel comfortable.

### 4. More is always best

Basically, I believe in bounty. I come from the school of "make sure there's enough so that if fifteen other people come by, you're set!" You don't have to follow my "exaggerated" food philosophy, but you always do want to have a bit more than just enough. You'll notice that I have recipes for six here. These would be perfect for four—with leftovers. The bottom line is that I don't want people to feel that they shouldn't take more because there isn't enough.

### 5. Let guests sit where they like

Unless it's a formal dinner for a business meeting or other special occasion, I never have assigned seating. I believe that this is the way to go when you're having friends over. It makes the atmosphere more relaxed. And finally:

**6. Enjoy yourself!**

The more relaxed you are, the better your guests will feel. Creating a calm and welcoming atmosphere should be one of your top priorities.

Breaking bread with friends and family is one of the most enjoyable and natural things that we do in life. I hope these pages create lots of delicious—and fun—memories for you and your loved ones!

# Wines of Abruzzo

When we were growing up, our families all made their own wine. The grapes were shipped from our cousins in California or the local distributor. This was always a community event (which would explain the incredible number of fruit flies in my neighborhood!). My dad would use and then loan out his grape press, as well as offer free consultations about the lunar cycle and when to add sulfites. This traditional process, which he swears by, was successful year after year.

But it wasn't only the grown-ups who were involved in the wine-making event; they got the kids involved, too—and we developed a taste, early on, for that special nectar. I remember that even at a very young age, during the summer, my grandfather would treat us to slices of our homegrown peaches, gently dipped in his homemade wine. (Talk about wine pairing!) They would also use the wine in other ways. For example, my *nonna* and mother would make a wine reduction with honey, and use it for glazing holiday cookies. To this day, my mother carries on the tradition.

Wine is a key player when it comes to enjoying this cuisine, so I'm presenting a wonderful collection to you. My dear friend Jocelyn Klemm was very helpful and summarized the many attributes and characteristics of wines from Abruzzo. Like me, Jocelyn feels that you should be informed, but let your tastes, as opposed to trends, dictate which wines you enjoy. So, if you don't particularly enjoy white wine, choose a red that will complement your dish (and vice versa). Though we've suggested wines that match the meals, we encourage you to explore and experiment.

In every region of Italy, the foods and wines of the land have evolved together, so that when friends and family gather for a meal, there's a natural fit between what is on the plate and what is in the glass. The wines of Abruzzo are as flavorful and as versatile as its local ingredients and dishes.

L'Aquila is situated in genuine wine country, within the province of Abruzzo, between the sea and the mountains. Abruzzo's terrain is blessed with ideal natural conditions for grape growing, nestled at the foot of the Apennines and extending to the Adriatic coastline. Its hilly slopes are covered in vines, and the high altitude vineyards benefit from sunshine, cooling breezes, and a mild climate. This results in rich yet not overly heavy wines. Also, the rocky soil forces the roots of the grapevines to grow deep, so that each grape reflects the complex minerality of the earth in which it's grown.

Though not as well known as Tuscany or Veneto, Abruzzo places fifth in terms of production among Italy's wine regions. And while the flagship Montepulciano d'Abruzzo has a reputation as a mass market wine, this prolific, plump and juicy grape makes good, even great, wines, with its deep color, lower acidity, and soft, sweet tannins.

Abruzzo wine styles range from dry "still" wines (*bianco*/white, *rosso*/red, or *rosato*/rosé) to sweet *passito* (dessert) wines. The wines feature indigenous grapes of the region: Montepulciano, Trebbiano, Pecorino, Passerina, Malvasia, and Cococciola, as well as international varietals like Chardonnay, Merlot, and Cabernet Sauvignon.

In white wine, Trebbiano d'Abruzzo is most prominent: a light, neutral wine with higher acidity. This wine can be made with different varieties of Trebbiano grapes, so if you can find wines made with the true Trebbiano d'Abruzzo (rather than the more common Trebbiano Toscana), they will have much more of a fruit character and flavor. The refreshing quality of Trebbiano d'Abruzzo makes it a lovely wine to start a meal, with antipasti or with salads.

The red wines of Abruzzo are distinctive. The Montepulciano grape is the base for Montepulciano d'Abruzzo, the top red wine of the region. In fact, Montepulciano's roots can be traced to L'Aquila's Peligna Valley, as far back as the eighteenth century. This grape is cultivated in all four provinces of Abruzzo: Chieti, L'Aquila, Pescara, and Teramo.

Montepulciano d'Abruzzo comes in two main styles of red wines. The first is young, fresh-tasting, robust, fruity, and uncomplicated. Typically this style is meant to be consumed within 6 to 18 months of the vintage. The wine will have a minimum content of 85% of Montepulciano grapes; up to 15% other red wine grapes may be added to the blend. Because these young wines are rich and juicy, but not too tannic, they marry well with pasta dishes, light meats like pork and veal, and even some of the fish dishes of the region.

The second style of Montepulciano d'Abruzzo has more intensity of fruit, is more concentrated, and is often oak-aged. When labeled "Riserva," these wines were aged for a minimum twenty-four months before their release, of which at least nine months must have been in oak.

These more powerful wines, with aromas of black cherry and cocoa, have a velvety texture and succulent, savory taste. With their rich, full-bodied qualities, these wines stand up to grilled lamb and roast meat dishes, typical of the cuisine of L'Aquila.

There's a third style of wine made with Montepulciano, the appealing rosé wine Cerasuolo, named for its cherry-red color. This rich, dry rosé is made by soaking the Montepulciano grape juice with its skins for just a few hours, enough time to pick up color and aromas. The wine, with its aromas of cherries, strawberries, and a touch of almonds on the finish, is a versatile choice with most antipasti, vegetable dishes, fish, and light meats.

At the end of the meal, dessert in a glass comes in the form of *passito* wines. These wines are made by picking and drying grape bunches, either on trays or by hanging from rafters, for many months. The sugars in the "raisined" grapes become concentrated, and when fermented, result in a naturally sweet wine. *Passito* wines may be *bianco* (made from Trebbiano, Passerina, and Malvasia) or *rosso* (made from Montepulciano). Aromas in *passito* wines are more like dried-fruit versions of still wines made from the same grapes: dried tropical fruit in *passito bianco* and dried black cherries in *passito rosso*. They pair well with biscotti or with fruity desserts like *crostata*.

Whether you pair your meal with a glass of wine from Abruzzo or with something from closer to home, raise a glass to the marriage of good food and wine!

## Trattoria San Biagio
Watercolor Painting
by Renée Angela Filice

In the fall of 2006, my cousin Renée, who lives in California, met me at JFK Airport and off we went to Italy. There I shared L'Aquila—such an important part of my life—with her. Together we strolled down the streets, stopped by my favorite coffee bar near Piazza Duomo. We would buy our freshly made *panini*, and sit in the park next to the medieval Basilica of Santa Maria di Collemaggio, one of L'Aquila's beautiful sites.

Of course we also visited my favorite trattoria San Biagio. Renée, who is an artist with a talent for painting on silk, was also inspired by the restaurant's warm hospitality! She took some photos and later recreated the image in this beautiful painting, which now hangs in my home in the country. I will cherish it forever.

BREAKING BREAD ON *Monday*

ANTIPASTI

# Bruschetta

What's not to love about bruschetta? Using nice, crusty Italian bread as a bed for fresh tomatoes, garlic, basil, and olive oil makes this a treat that's as delicious to taste as it is to behold. Though you can use fresh bread, you can also toast up any remaining stale bread. You have the option of toasting it in an oven or on a grill.

**Serves 6**

12 two-inch slices of Italian bread
4 medium red, yellow, or heirloom tomatoes, cut into ¼-inch cubes
3 cloves garlic: 2 minced, 1 whole
10 fresh basil leaves, sliced into ribbons
1 to 2 teaspoons coarse salt
¼ teaspoon fresh ground black pepper
2 tablespoons extra virgin olive oil

Preheat the oven to 375°F.

In a medium-sized bowl, combine the tomatoes, minced garlic, olive oil, basil, salt, and pepper. Stir to combine and set aside.

Toast the bread by placing the bread slices on a sheet pan and bake until golden on both sides (about 7 minutes).

Using whole clove of garlic, lightly rub one side of each slice of bread. Top with a spoonful of the tomato mixture.

Plate and serve.

PRIMI PIATTI

# Pasta e Fagioli (Pasta and Beans)

This is a hearty and beautifully fragrant dish. Traditionally made with garbanzo beans, I sometimes prefer its less dense cousin: the red kidney bean. (You can even use canned red kidney beans if you're in a hurry, but please rinse them well!) I use the delightful corkscrew-shaped *cellentani* or the circular *orecchiette*, Italian for "little ears." This dish is perfect to serve on a brisk fall day, with a green leafy salad and your favorite crusty bread. Don't forget to throw in a few red chilis for good luck!

**Serves 6**

1½ cups dry garbanzos (or canned, drained and rinsed)
2 teaspoons salt
1 pound orecchiette pasta
1 clove garlic, coarsely chopped
1 sprig rosemary, leaves removed
2 tablespoons extra virgin olive oil
Freshly grated Parmigiano cheese, to taste

Soak the beans in water overnight. Drain and reserve beans. Place them in a pot with enough water to cover them by an inch or so, and bring to a boil. Add salt and lower the heat to medium. Keep simmering until the beans are tender but not mushy. This could be as short as 30 minutes or as long as an hour, depending on the beans used. (If you are using canned beans, you can add them direction to the cooked pasta.)

Using a large pot, cook the pasta according to the package instructions until it is al dente. Reserve one cup of water.

In a large pan, sauté the garlic and the rosemary in the olive oil over medium heat. Add the pasta and beans and toss together, while adding the reserved pasta water until the dish has achieved the desired consistency. It should be creamy and not dried out.

Sprinkle with Parmigiano and serve immediately.

PRIMI PIATTI

# Pasta con Salsa di Maiale (Pasta with a Pork Tomato Sauce)

Bucatini, a kind of dense pasta that looks like spaghetti with a hole in the middle, is perfect for heartier sauces like this one. If you can't find bucatini, don't worry! Any *penne*, *ziti*, or *rigatoni* will do just fine. Any cut of fresh pork: shoulder, ribs, or sausage will also work.

**Serves 6**

1 pound boneless pork, about ½-inch thick, cubed
2 tablespoons extra virgin olive oil
1 medium onion, finely chopped
2 teaspoons coarse salt
¼ teaspoon fresh ground black pepper
½ cup dry white wine
4 medium tomatoes, coarsely chopped or canned (16 ounces)
Hot chili pepper (or red chili flakes) to taste
1 pound bucatini pasta
Freshly grated pecorino cheese

Heat the olive oil in a sauté pan over medium heat. Add the onions and sauté for several minutes until they start to soften. Add the pork and season with salt and black pepper. Let it brown evenly on both sides for 15 minutes. Add the wine, tomatoes, and chili pepper flakes and continue to simmer until the pork is cooked through, for an hour.

Using a large pot, cook the pasta according to the package instructions until it is al dente. Immediately toss with the sauce until it is well coated. Serve on a platter and sprinkle with freshly grated pecorino cheese.

SECONDI PIATTI

# Cotolette di Vitello (Veal Cutlets)

I have always loved thin, tender, moist, and delectable veal cutlets, both for dinner and for sandwiches the next day—if we were lucky enough to have leftovers. This basic recipe can work for veal or chicken, and should be served with your favorite pasta or potato dish and a leafy green salad.

**Serves 6**

6 veal cutlets, pounded to ⅛-inch thickness
4 tablespoons all-purpose flour
3 large eggs, lightly beaten
1 cup bread crumbs (unseasoned)
Salt and fresh ground black pepper, to taste
½ cup vegetable or extra virgin olive oil

Season the cutlets with salt and pepper on both sides. Arrange three plates side-by-side for the flour, eggs, and bread. Dip the cutlets in the flour, coating both sides, and shake off any excess. Then dip them in the egg mixture and, finally, coat them in the bread crumbs.

Place a large frying pan over medium heat and add the oil. Cook the cutlets in batches until cooked through and golden brown on both sides. If you are cooking in batches, you may want to keep the cutlets warm in a low-temperature oven until you're ready to serve. Place on paper towels to absorb the excess fat.

Serve warm.

CONTORNI

# Insalata con Scaglie di Parmigiano

## (Romaine Lettuce Salad with Shaved Parmigiano Cheese)

This salad works beautifully at the beginning or the end of the meal. I sometimes substitute the dressing's balsamic vinegar with red wine vinegar or fresh lemon juice. If you are like me and love anchovies, add a couple more to your dish.

**Serves 6**

2 heads romaine lettuce
1 cup cherry tomatoes, halved
3 tablespoons extra virgin olive oil
1 tablespoon balsamic vinegar
1 clove garlic, finely chopped
1 small can anchovies (optional)
Shavings of fresh Parmigiano cheese, to taste
½ teaspoon salt
¼ teaspoon fresh ground black pepper

Clean and tear the romaine lettuce into small, bite-sized chunks and place in a salad bowl. Add the tomatoes.

In a separate bowl, whisk together the olive oil, garlic, and balsamic vinegar. Let the vinaigrette rest for 1 minute.

Just before serving, pour the vinaigrette on top of the lettuce and tomatoes, and mix well. Top with the anchovies, if you wish, and parmigiano shavings. Add salt and pepper to taste, but keep in mind that the cheese and anchovies are quite salty.

CONTORNI

# Verdure Rustiche con Riduzione di Aceto Balsamico
(Rustic Vegetables with Balsamic Reduction)

Any vegetable drizzled with extra virgin olive oil, tossed with garlic, and sprinkled with chilies is perfect with meat or fish—or even on its own! A drizzle of the balsamic reduction, which you may find other uses for, complements the vegetables and adds a sweet touch that beautifully balances the spiciness. I try to use vegetables that are in season. Try grilling some of the vegetables, they are delicious!

**Serves 6**

*For the vegetables*
1 pound medium new potatoes (approximately 4 to 6), scrubbed and cut into chunks
2 cups chopped endive (or kale, spinach, or Swiss chard)
2 cups sliced zucchini
2 cups green beans, trimmed
3 to 4 tablespoons extra virgin olive oil
2 cloves garlic, sliced
4 medium tomatoes, chopped
1 teaspoon red chili flakes
Salt

*For the balsamic reduction*
1 cup balsamic vinegar
1 tablespoon honey
1 bay leaf
3 whole cloves garlic (optional)

*For the balsamic reduction:*
Pour the balsamic vinegar into a saucepan over medium-low heat. Stir in the honey, bay leaf, and garlic cloves. Cook over low heat, stirring from time to time, for about 30 minutes or until the vinegar has reduced by half and reaches a syrupy consistency. Pour the syrup through a strainer, and remove the bay leaf and garlic.

*For the vegetables:*
Bring a large pot half-filled with water to a boil. Add the potatoes and 2 tablespoons of salt, and cook for 15 minutes. Then add endive, zucchini, and beans, and cook for another 3 minutes, or until the vegetables are fork tender.

Heat the olive oil in a large skillet over medium heat. Add the red chili flakes and garlic, and sauté until the garlic is golden.

Drain the cooked vegetables. Add them, along with the tomatoes, to the skillet. Add salt and continue cooking, stirring frequently, for about two minutes. Drizzle the vinegar reduction over the vegetables just before serving.

DOLCI

# Biscotti Amaretti (Amaretti Cookies)

Anyone who knows Italian sweets knows that amaretti are quite popular. These cookies, which can also be made with my other favorite, hazelnuts, are perfect after a meal with a bit of espresso. Also, they freeze well, so you can make them ahead of time and then take them out an hour before serving. These are my mother's signature cookies. Instead of parchment paper, she usually sprinkles the baking sheets with flour. I'm still trying to master them!

**Makes about 3 dozen**

3 cups almonds (with skins), plus an additional 36 whole almonds
1 cup white granulated sugar
2 large eggs
1 teaspoon almond extract
2 cups of confectioner's sugar, spread on 12 inches of wax paper (for rolling)

Preheat the oven to 350°F.

Lightly grease three baking sheets with vegetable spray or line with parchment paper.

Using a food processor, pulse the 3 cups of almonds until they are finely ground. In a separate bowl, beat eggs, sugar, and almond extract. Add the ground nuts and gently fold them together until you have a moist mixture that you can form into balls.

Using a teaspoon or your fingers, scoop up the batter and form balls, and then roll them in the confectioner's sugar. Place the balls at least an inch apart on the greased baking sheet. Prior to baking, press one almond into each ball.

Bake for about 15 minutes or until the cookies are golden in color and firm to the touch.

Let them cool before removing them from the baking sheets.

BREAKING BREAD ON *Tuesday*

ANTIPASTI

# Prosciutto e Melone (Prosciutto with Melon)

Prosciutto with melon was served at many meals in my home, not just for special occasions. This simple and elegant appetizer, which offers the perfect contrast of sweet and salty, was also one of Paul's favorites. In fact, he ate it at any time (not just as an appetizer!). My dad used to make this dish with his own prosciutto, slightly thicker. I prefer the thinner slices, but insist on excellent-quality prosciutto (like Parma). If you prefer, you can use honeydew melon instead of cantaloupe. I also love the pairing with fresh figs and prosciutto with a drizzle of honey. Now that's amore!

**Serves 6**

1 ripe cantaloupe, peeled, seeded, and cut into ½-inch thick slices
¾ pound paper-thin prosciutto slices, cut into 1-inch-wide strips (about 6 inches in length)
4 to 6 lettuce leaves (for garnish)

On a large platter, create a bed of lettuce leaves. I refer to them as "lettuce ruffles."

Wrap each melon slice with a prosciutto strip. The strip should wrap the melon slice several times.

Place the prepared melon slices over the lettuce and serve immediately. You can also cover and refrigerate the prepared dish (up to 2 hours) before serving.

PRIMI PIATTI

# Minestra di Farro (Spelt Soup)

This hearty soup, which is really more stew-like than your usual soup, is quick and delicious as a first course or wonderful lunch. There are many variations of this ancient wheat grain. You will need to refer to the package instructions for specific cooking directions. Make sure you serve it immediately because the spelt continues to absorb liquid—you'll lose your "soup" if you don't serve it right away! You can also make this with barley.

**Serves 6**

1 cup spelt (available in some supermarkets and specialty stores)
2 tablespoons extra virgin olive oil
4 ounces pancetta (or bacon), cut in ¼-inch-thick pieces
1 medium onion, chopped
1 clove garlic, minced
4 medium tomatoes, diced
2 tablespoons chopped fresh Italian flat leaf parsley
1 tablespoon chopped fresh basil
Freshly grated pecorino cheese
Salt and fresh ground black pepper, to taste
½ cup freshly grated pecorina cheese

Prepare the spelt according to the package instructions. (Some brands may require soaking overnight.) Drain spelt and reserve two cups of water.

In the meantime, heat the olive oil over medium-high heat. Saute the pancetta, onion, and garlic. After 5 minutes, when the onion has started to soften, add the tomatoes, parsley, and basil. Lower the heat to medium and simmer for 10 minutes. Add salt and pepper. Stir in the drained spelt and two cups of the reserved water. Remove from heat and add the pecorino cheese to the soup and stir throughout. Serve immediately.

PRIMI PIATTI

# Spaghetti al Pomodoro (Spaghetti with Tomato Sauce)

This dish is a perfect example of less being more. The combination of these seven ingredients is simply delicious. I love the San Marzano tomatoes. You don't need to use spaghetti; you could use any type of pasta except *capellini*, which is far too light for this sauce. In general you should use a heavier pasta with a heavier sauce! This is a basic "go to" sauce for so many other dishes.

**Serves 6**

1 pound spaghetti
2 to 3 tablespoons extra virgin olive oil
2 carrots, finely diced
1 large onion, finely diced
1 to 2 cloves garlic, finely chopped
5 to 6 medium tomatoes, diced, or canned (16 ounces)
1 teaspoon salt
¼ teaspoon fresh ground black pepper
1 teaspoon red chili flakes (optional)
Freshly grated Parmigiano cheese

Heat a large sauté pan over medium and add the oil. Then add the carrots and onions and cook until they start to soften, about 5 minutes. Add the garlic. Stir in the tomatoes and salt and pepper. Cook the sauce for about 10 minutes. The red chili flakes are optional; if your guests do not like their pasta spicy, simply serve the chili flakes at the table and then your guests can add their own.

Using a large pot, cook the pasta according to the package instructions until it is al dente. Drain and toss with tomato sauce.

Sprinkle with Parmigiano and serve.

SECONDI PIATTI

# Baccalà al Forno (Baked Salt Cod)

Don't be deterred by the appearance of dried salt cod. I promise you will love this sumptuous meal! *Baccalà*, often called the poor man's fish because of its price and the fact that it's so easy to keep, can be easily re-hydrated into this popular, tender, and delicate dish. Prior to cooking your *baccalà*, be sure to soak it for about two days in water (changing the water regularly) to help remove most of the salt. My grandmother would sometimes add potatoes to her *baccalà*. Either way, I'm sure you will enjoy this combination of flavors.

**Serves 6**

2 pounds *baccalà* (salt cod), soaked in water that is changed 3 to 4 times over 48 hours, well drained
1 cup all-purpose flour (for dredging)
¼ cup extra virgin olive oil
2 medium white onions, chopped
2 cloves garlic, coarsely chopped
One 28-ounce can San Marzano tomatoes, coarsely chopped
1 teaspoon red chili flakes
1 tablespoon capers (in salt or brine)
1 tablespoon dried oregano
½ cup red wine
½ cup chopped fresh Italian flat parsley, for garnish
Salt and fresh ground black pepper, to taste

Preheat the oven to 350°F.

Drain the water. Cut the *baccalà* into large pieces and pat it dry with paper towels. Dredge the fish in the flour, making sure both sides are evenly—but lightly—coated. Shake off extra flour prior to frying. Heat the oil in an oven-proof frying pan over medium heat. Fry the cod on both sides until brown, about two minutes on each side. Add the chopped onions and garlic, and sauté for about 3 minutes or until they start to soften. The salted capers should be rinsed before adding. Add the tomatoes, red chili flakes, capers, oregano, and red wine. Simmer uncovered, stirring occasionally, for 10 minutes. Season with salt and pepper to taste. Place the pan in the oven, cover, and bake for 20 minutes. Remove the pan, add fresh parsley, and serve immediately.

SECONDI PIATTI

# Peperoni Arrostiti Ripieni con Salsiccia

(Roasted Stuffed Peppers with Sausage)

Roasted vegetables are great, both as vessels for all kinds of ingredients and for creating one-pot meals. My mother and grandmother would stuff zucchini, potatoes, eggplant, and tomatoes, usually from our garden (or whatever was on sale at the store). The stuffing also depended on what they had available. Though I have chosen bread and sausage for this recipe, they also used rice—or even just bread crumbs. I have used stale Italian bread and whole wheat. You are not restricted to a specific type of bread. The point is, you can be creative. Use whatever you have on hand and your family enjoys!

**Serves 6**

6 bell peppers (red, green, or yellow)
2 tablespoons extra virgin olive oil
1½ pounds (6 links) sweet and spicy sausage
2 cloves garlic, chopped
3 medium white onions, chopped
½ teaspoon red chili flakes
Salt and fresh ground black pepper, to taste
1 cup freshly grated Parmigiano cheese
2 eggs, lightly beaten
1 tablespoon fresh Italian flat leaf parsley
½ loaf of bread, cubed (between 3 and 4 cups)

Preheat the oven to 350°F.

Cut off the tops of each pepper so that there is a cavity to stuff, and set aside. Finely dice the pepper tops to add in with the rest of your stuffing.

In a large pan, heat 1 tablespoon of olive oil over medium heat. Remove the sausage from the casings and crumble the meat into pan. Let the meat brown, stirring occasionally, for about 8 minutes or until golden on all sides. Add the garlic, chopped onion, diced bell pepper tops, red chili flakes, salt, and pepper. Sauté for about 4 minutes, or until the onions and pepper start to soften. Remove from the heat and let sit for 5 minutes.

Drizzle 1 tablespoon olive oil in a large baking pan and place the peppers in the pan standing upright. Sprinkle a pinch of salt and pepper into the pepper cavities to season.

In a large bowl, whisk the eggs and add a pinch of salt, pepper, and parsley. Add the cubed bread, ½ cup of Parmigiano cheese, and toss lightly. Add the sausage mixture and mix well.

Gently fill each of the peppers with the mixture but don't pack the stuffing. Sprinkle remaining Parmigiano on top. Bake for 45 minutes, or until the peppers have softened and the stuffing is golden. Serve immediately.

CONTORNI

# *Rapini* (Broccoli Rabe)

A staple in many Italian homes, broccoli rabe (also referred to as rapini) offers the perfect balance to a pasta dinner. This slightly bitter vegetable can also be substituted with mustard greens, dandelion greens (another favorite in my house), or Chinese broccoli. One of my favorites is serving broccoli rabe with fresh sausage and lots of hot pepper. How can you tell I'm from Calabria?

**Serves 6**

2 bunches of rinsed and trimmed broccoli rabe
3 tablespoons extra virgin olive oil
1 clove garlic, sliced
Salt
Italian chili pepper (or red chili flakes)

Bring a large pot of water to boil and add 2 tablespoons of salt. Blanche the broccoli rabe—by dipping it into the boiling water—for about 5 minutes; this will remove some of the bitterness. Immediately transfer to an ice bath to retain the green color.

Drain well. Heat about 1 tablespoon of the oil in a large frying pan over medium heat. Add the garlic and sauté the broccoli rabe for several minutes until the stems are tender (but be careful not to overcook them). Drizzle the remaining oil on top. Add salt and chili pepper to taste.

DOLCI

# Crostata d'Albicocche (Rustic Apricot Fruit Tart)

Crostata, a typical Italian dessert tart, is perfect for those of us who are not such great bakers. It's so simple and easy. Plus it's flexible: you can make it with any of your favorite jams. The recipe provided uses a food processor, but you can use an electric hand mixer or even your hands.

**Serves 6**

2 tablespoons white granulated sugar
1¼ cups all-purpose flour
½ teaspoon salt
Zest of 1 lemon (about 1 tablespoon)
½ cup unsalted butter, chilled and cut into small cubes
¼ cup cold water
6 to 8 ounces fruit jam (apricot, fig, or orange marmalade all work well)
1 cup of sliced almonds (for decorating)

Preheat the oven to 400° F.

Using a food processor, combine the sugar, flour, salt, and lemon zest. Pulse about 10 times. Add the cubes of butter and process until the mixture becomes a crumbly dough. Very slowly, drizzle in enough water until the mixture forms a ball and pulls away from the sides. This should only take about 30 seconds. The dough will be slightly sticky.

On a very cold surface (marble is best), shape the dough into a flat disc. Try not to overwork it with your hands; this will give you a much flakier pastry. Wrap the dough in plastic wrap and chill in the refrigerator for about an hour.

Remove the dough and dust the surface lightly with flour. Working very quickly, roll it out to about an 11-inch round. This does not need to be a perfect circle because this is a very rustic type of pie. Transfer this to a parchment-lined baking sheet. Spread the center with a layer of your favorite store-bought or homemade jam. Gently fold up the sides and pleat the dough; this looks pretty and will prevent the jam from escaping.

Bake the *crostata* for about 30 minutes or until the edges are golden. Let cool for 10 minutes. Sprinkle sliced almonds around the edge.

BREAKING BREAD ON *Wednesday*

ANTIPASTI

# Insalata Caprese (Caprese Salad)

This classically colorful (red, white, and green) salad is perfect for any meal. This is one of my favorite antipasto. I've eaten this in other parts of Italy, and it is a popular dish. The sprinkles of fresh basil and oregano balance beautifully in taste, texture, and color with the fresh mozzarella (ideally served at room temperature) and ripe red tomatoes. Serve this as a side salad with the grilled lamb, or on its own with fresh, crusty Italian bread. You can substitute the mozzarella with buffalo mozzarella, or use bocconcini (little round balls of mozzarella) and toss with either grape or cherry tomatoes. This is a dish that you can make ahead of time.

**Serves 6**

3 medium red, yellow, or heirloom tomatoes
1 pound fresh mozzarella
3 to 4 tablespoons extra virgin olive oil
Salt and fresh ground black pepper, to taste
1 teaspoon dried oregano
12 fresh basil leaves

Slice 12 slices of each of tomatoes and fresh mozzarella into pieces that are approximately ¼-inch thick. They should be roughly the same size. Arrange them on a platter, alternating the slices of tomatoes with the slices of mozzarella cheese and basil leaves.

Drizzle the olive oil on top. Add the salt and pepper. Sprinkle the oregano on top.

Keep it at room temperature until you're ready to serve.

PRIMI PIATTI

# Minestra di Verdure con Riso (Vegetable Soup with Rice)

Certainly a meal on its own, this tasty soup is quite flexible in terms of ingredients and is great any time of year. As a first course, this is a lovely start; as a main course, serve with a salad (like the Caprese Salad on page 56) or with your favorite green salad and Italian bread. Homemade beef broth is ideal, but chicken or vegetable also work well. Here I've suggested topping the soup with Parmigiano or Romano cheese—although Paul used to love to add cubed chunks of fresh mozzarella!

**Serves 6**

2 tablespoons extra virgin olive oil
2 cloves garlic, minced
3 to 4 chopped celery stalks
2 sliced or chopped carrots
½ cup peas (fresh or frozen)
2 small plum tomatoes, chopped
½ cup fava beans (fresh or frozen)
3 to 4 stalks Swiss chard, cut into ½-inch chunks (you can also substitute with other leafy greens like spinach, escarole, or kale).
6 cups beef or chicken broth
1 cup rice (uncooked white or brown)
Salt and fresh ground black pepper, to taste
Freshly grated Parmigiano (optional)

In a large pot, heat and sauté garlic for one minute. Add the vegetables and cook for about 10 minutes, or until the vegetables start to soften and lightly brown. Add the broth and bring to a boil. Season with salt and pepper.

Add the rice, lower to a simmer, cover, and cook until the rice is tender, about 20 minutes.

Sprinkle with Parmigiano and serve immediately.

PRIMI PIATTI

# Pasta al Forno con Pomodori e Capperi

*(Baked Pasta with Tomatoes and Capers)*

The salty capers and the sweet tomatoes marry beautifully in this pasta dish, which can be made with any of your favorite short pastas: elbow macaroni, *gemelli*, *campanelle*, *penne*, *ziti*, or *radiatore*. But what really stands out in this sauce are the flavors of the oven-roasted tomatoes, which make it a "*delizioso*" change from traditional tomato sauce.

**Serves 6**

1 pound of *rigatoncini* pasta
5 large red beefsteak tomatoes
½ cup fresh coarsely chopped basil leaves
2 cloves garlic, minced
2 tablespoons capers (in salt or brine)
1 cup bread crumbs (unseasoned)
1 pinch dried oregano
Salt and fresh ground black pepper, to taste
4 tablespoons extra virgin olive oil
Freshly grated Parmigiano cheese (optional)

Preheat the oven to 350°F.

Dice the tomatoes into medium pieces. In a small bowl, combine the chopped basil, minced garlic, and capers. The salted capers should be rinsed before adding. Mix well and set aside. Using some of the olive oil, grease a 9-by-13 inch baking dish. Spread the bottom of the pan with the tomatoes in a single layer. Next, layer the garlic, basil, and capers. Sprinkle the bread crumbs on top. Add the oregano and a pinch of salt. Evenly drizzle the remaining oil on top. Bake for about 30 minutes, stirring at least once, until the tomatoes have softened.

Using a large pot, cook the pasta according to the package instructions until it is al dente. Drain and stir into the baked tomato mixture. Combine well, and return the dish to the oven for another 5 minutes until golden and bubbling. Sprinkle with Parmigiano to taste. Serve warm.

SECONDI PIATTI

# Costolette d'Agnello alla Griglia (Grilled Lamb Chops)

Anyone who is familiar with L'Aquila knows that lamb dominates the meat scene in this mountainous region. Like many of the local dishes, this one is totally unpretentious and elegant in its simplicity. I confess: I'm a huge lamb fan, too! Grilled lamb is beautifully combined with any pasta dish, or the Boiled Potatoes with Parsley dish on page 66, and a leafy green salad.

**Serves 6**

12 rib lamb chops
1 tablespoon coarse salt
½ teaspoon fresh ground black pepper
Rosemary leaves to sprinkle on the chops before serving, plus sprigs to garnish the plate
Extra virgin olive oil

Heat a grill or a grill pan over high heat until almost smoking. Salt and pepper both sides of the lamb. Add the chops and sear for about 2 minutes. Flip the chops over and cook for another 3 minutes (for medium-rare) or 3½ to 4 minutes (for medium).

Let the lamb rest for about 5 minutes prior to serving. Sprinkle rosemary on the lamb and add a drizzle of extra virgin olive oil.

CONTORNI

# Carciofi al Forno *(Baked Artichokes)*

As much as I love artichokes, many times—when I'm in a rush—I don't use the fresh vegetable but instead just reach for the cans in my pantry. Okay, ideally we would use all of this incredibly prehistoric looking "flower," but even with canned artichokes this dish is wonderfully delicious and works well. Truth be told, I could eat these as a meal with a salad! Perfect as a side dish for grilled meat or fish, this simpler version of baked artichokes is a treat that you and your guests will enjoy.

**Serves 6**

2 cans artichoke hearts, drained (8½ ounces each)
2 large eggs
1 cup bread crumbs (unseasoned)
2 tablespoons finely chopped fresh Italian flat leaf parsley
2 tablespoons freshly grated Parmigiano cheese
3 to 4 tablespoons extra virgin olive oil
½ teaspoon salt
¼ teaspoon fresh ground black pepper
Zest of 1 lemon (about 1 tablespoon)

Preheat the oven to 400°F.

Drain and rinse the artichokes. Pat them dry. Lightly beat the eggs in a small bowl. In another bowl, combine the bread crumbs, salt, pepper, and cheese. Dip the artichokes in the egg mixture, making sure they are evenly coated. Then coat them well in the bread-crumb mixture.

Grease the bottom of a baking pan with about 2 tablespoons of olive oil. Place the artichokes in the pan. Sprinkle any remaining bread crumbs over the artichokes.

Drizzle the remaining olive oil over the artichokes. Bake for about 20 minutes. The artichokes should be warmed through, and the bread-crumb mixture should be toasted.

Sprinkle with parsley and lemon zest before serving.

CONTORNI

# Patate Lesse con Prezzemolo Fresco

(Boiled Potatoes with Fresh Parsley)

This simple side dish is not only comforting, but it's also a great mate for most grilled meat and fish. Though my favorite is Yukon gold, I also like the look and the taste of a variety of potatoes, so don't be afraid to mix it up. Leftover idea: Add roasted peppers, green olives, and tuna (packed in oil) to the potatoes and serve over a bed of lettuce for a perfect lunch.

**Serves 6**

1 pound small new potatoes (approximately 10 to 12)
4 tablespoons extra virgin olive oil
2 tablespoons red wine vinegar
Salt and fresh ground black pepper, to taste
2 tablespoons finely chopped fresh Italian flat leaf parsley

Place the potatoes in a medium-sized pot. Cover them with cold water, the water level should be about 1 inch above the potatoes, and bring to a boil. Simmer until they're cooked through but not mushy, approximately 20 minutes. You can check them by inserting a fork or a knife. They are done when you don't feel any resistance as you press through the center.

When they are cooked, drain the water. Once they're cool enough to handle, cut them into 1-inch cubes. Toss them with the olive oil, vinegar, salt, and pepper while they are still warm so that they can drink in all the dressing. Taste and adjust the seasoning as desired. Place them on a serving dish and sprinkle them with the parsley.

Serve warm or at room temperature.

DOLCI

# Torta di Mele (Apple Cake)

The first time I made this in New York, the bittersweet chocolate I found to cut and put in this luscious cake had almonds in it. Now, I don't know if I would make it without the nuts. Still, the contrast between the bittersweet chocolate and the flavor of the lemon-kissed apples is just amazing—not to mention the background of the rich, moist cake. Perfect for dessert any time, this apple cake is also great reheated (just enough to melt the chocolate) in the morning with a cup of coffee.

**Serves 6**

3 Granny Smith apples (or your favorite)
1 lemon
5 eggs, separated
1 cup white granulated sugar
1 cup vegetable or canola oil
1½ cups all-purpose flour
1½ teaspoons baking soda
4 to 5 ounces bittersweet chocolate, with or without nuts, chopped
Confectioner's sugar (optional)

Preheat the oven to 325°F.

Grease a 9-inch (1-inch deep) glass pie plate.

Peel and core the apples. Cut them into ¼-inch thick slices and place them in a bowl. Squeeze the fresh lemon juice on top and mix to coat. Let them sit for a few minutes.

In a bowl, beat the egg whites until stiff, then set aside. In a separate bowl, beat the egg yolks with the sugar. Add oil and mix until well blended. Combine the flour and baking soda, and slowly add them to the wet mixture. Fold in the egg whites and mix until well blended. Pour half the batter into the prepared pan. Evenly spread the apple slices on top. Top them with the chopped chocolate.

Pour the rest of the batter on top. Bake for approximately 40 minutes or until a toothpick inserted into the center comes out clean.

Cool the cake and sprinkle with confectioner's sugar, if desired.

BREAKING BREAD ON *Thursday*

ANTIPASTI

# Melanzane alla Griglia con Olive e Basilico

(Grilled Eggplant with Cured Black Olives and Basil)

Don't be intimidated by eggplant! This is one of my favorite vegetables, and I enjoy it whether it's in eggplant Parmigiana, or simply oven-roasted on its own. This very simple antipasto is perfect as part of a lunch with a salad or as a starter for almost any of the dinners in this collection.

**Serves 6**

2 medium eggplants
4 tablespoons extra virgin olive oil
2 cloves garlic, finely minced
1 pinch of dried oregano
1 pinch of red chili flakes
Salt and fresh ground black pepper, to taste
6 to 8 fresh basil leaves, coarsely chopped
18 small black cured olives

Heat a grill pan or a grill to medium high. Meanwhile, slice the eggplant into ½-inch thick slices (leave the skin on) and add salt and pepper to each side. Combine 3 tablespoons olive oil and garlic in a small bowl. Brush both sides of the eggplant slices with the garlic oil. Add the oregano and the red chili flakes.

Place the eggplant on the hot preheated grill. Grill for about 10 to 12 minutes, turning each side once after 5 to 6 minutes, until the eggplant is cooked (tender but not too mushy).

Place the eggplant on a platter. Sprinkle with the basil, drizzle the remaining olive oil, and add 2 to 3 olives on top of each slice.

PRIMI PIATTI

# Gnocchi al Sugo di Pomodoro (Gnocchi with Tomato Sauce)

Gnocchi, the Italian version of dumplings, come in many varieties, but this is one of the classic interpretations (though I also like the spinach and ricotta very much). My mother used to make them from leftover mashed potatoes, which was a great way to recreate one day's leftovers as the next day's main dish. (Actually both Mom and Nonna—my grandma—were great at that!) I sometimes think this is where the flavored gnocchi concept came from. Though I enjoy making these, I reach for the frozen version when I'm in a pinch.

**Serves 6**

2 pounds of starchy potatoes, peeled and cubed
3 tablespoons salt
¾ cup grated pecorino cheese
1 egg, lightly beaten
2 cups unbleached all-purpose flour, plus additional as needed
2 cups tomato sauce (see page 44)

Fill a large pot with cold water and the potatoes. Bring the water to a boil and add 1 tablespoon of salt. Make sure the water is well salted at this stage (taste it!). Cook the potatoes until tender (approximately 30 minutes) and drain.

Mash the potatoes using a ricer or food mill and let them cool for several minutes. Once the potatoes are cool enough to handle, use your hand or a wooden spoon to combine the potatoes with the flour, ½ cup of the grated cheese, and the egg. Form the dough into a ball, adding flour as needed. The dough should be pliable but not too sticky. Divide the dough into smaller balls (about the size of golf balls.) Roll each piece into a rope-like cylinder about the thickness of a thumb and cut into ¾-inch-long pieces.

To shape the gnocchi, dip a fork in flour (to prevent sticking) and hold it in one hand while pressing the gnocchi against the tines of the fork with the other hand. This takes a bit of practice at first. Place the formed gnocchi on a tea towel and dust them very lightly with flour so that they don't stick.

Bring a large pot of water to boil and add 2 tablespoons of salt. Make sure the pot is big enough not to overcrowd the gnocchi. Cook them until they float to the surface. Drain and toss them with your tomato sauce, and sprinkle with the remaining grated cheese.

PRIMI PIATTI

# Pasta con Funghi (Pasta with Mushrooms)

Mushrooms are another ubiquitous ingredient in the L'Aquila region, especially the porcini mushroom. I like to buy them fresh but always have the dried ones in my pantry. Be creative and use your favorite pasta shape! I like to combine them with other mushrooms. They are beautifully combined in this dish with the rich flavors of cream, butter, and cheese. It's not a typical dish, but what's great about simple and rustic is adding your own personal favorites. Ah! What could be bad about this combo?

**Serves 6**

2 pounds assorted fresh mushrooms (porcini or baby bellas), clean with stems trimmed, and dice into ½-inch thick chunks
1 pound spaghetti
2 tablespoons extra virgin olive oil
4 cloves garlic, minced
1 teaspoon salt
¼ teaspoon fresh ground pepper
2 tablespoons salted butter
1 cup freshly grated Parmigiano cheese
½ cup half-and-half cream

Heat the oil in a large pan over medium-high heat. Add the mushrooms and garlic and stir. Add salt and pepper. Reduce the heat to medium, cover the pan, and continue cooking, stirring occasionally, for approximately 4 minutes. Uncover the pan, add the butter, and cook the mushrooms for another 5 minutes, until golden brown. Add the half-and-half and then turn off the heat.

Using a large pot, cook the pasta according to the package instructions until it is al dente. Drain the pasta, but reserve 1 cup of the pasta water. Add the mushroom mixture and slowly add as much of the reserved water as required until the pasta is creamy.

Sprinkle the Parmigiano, toss and serve.

SECONDI PIATTI

# Maiale all'Arancia (Orange Glazed Pork)

Depending on the appetite of your crowd and what else you will be serving, you may want to double this recipe as it really allows for one chop per person. This orange-scented pork is perfect served with the Arugula Salad (page 130).

**Serves 6**

2 cups freshly squeezed orange juice
6 center-cut loin pork chops, about 1 inch thick, trimmed of excess fat
2 tablespoons extra virgin olive oil
½ cup dry white wine
2 oranges, cut into ¼-inch-thick slices
2 cloves garlic, minced
Coarse salt and fresh ground black pepper, to taste
1 tablespoon orange zest for garnish

Orange glaze: cook orange juice in a saucepan over a medium heat for about 10 minutes until it is reduced by half and there is about a cup of glaze. Set aside.

Sprinkle the chops with salt and pepper. Heat 2 tablespoons of oil in a large skillet over medium-high heat for 2 or 3 minutes. Add the chops (you'll probably have to cook them in batches, and it is important not to overcrowd the pan) and turn the heat to high. Cook the chops for 3 to 4 minutes on each side until they are brown.

Reduce the heat to medium. Add the wine and garlic and cook until the wine is almost evaporated, about 3 minutes. Add the orange glaze and sliced oranges, and reduce the heat to low. Cover and simmer for 10 to 15 minutes, turning once or twice until the chops are tender but not dry.

Remove the chops to a serving platter. Continue cooking the pan juices, stirring and scraping the bottom of the pan, until the liquid is reduced slightly. If you need to add more liquid, add a bit more orange juice combined with water or chicken stock. Pour over the chops, top with the orange zest, and serve.

SECONDI PIATTI

# Scaloppine al Vino Bianco

## (Veal Scaloppine in White Wine)

Veal scaloppine is a very simple and elegant dish to prepare. Believe it or not, the secret is in the flour. The flour helps brown the meat in minutes. It also gives the sauce a nice creamy texture. This is a very versatile dish, and you can use this secret with other meats. I also like using *Marsala* wine or fresh lemon juice as an alternate.

**Serves 6**

6 veal cutlets, thinly sliced (about 1½ pounds total)
1 cup all-purpose flour
⅓ cup extra virgin olive oil for frying
½ cup white wine
3 tablespoons salted butter
Salt and fresh ground black pepper, to taste

Sprinkle the flour evenly onto a plate or work surface. Lightly add salt and fresh black pepper on both sides of the cutlets, and then evenly dredge them with the flour.

Heat the olive oil in a large pan over medium. Add the prepared cutlets (you will probably have to do this in two batches, so divide the ingredients evenly) and cook them for only a few minutes, until tender and browned on both sides.

Add the wine. When the wine has almost reduced, add the butter and coat the cutlets.

Serve warm.

CONTORNI

# Finocchio e Cipolle Caramellizate con Scorza d'Arancia

## (Caramelized Fennel and Onions with Orange Rind)

Fennel is a favorite ingredient in many of our meals. In fact, it's often eaten raw, as a kind of palate cleanser and digestive, after eating dinner. This very versatile vegetable, which has a mild licorice flavor, combines beautifully with orange and is perfect with the other Thursday main dishes (pork on page 78 and veal on page 80) or with any meat or fish.

**Serves 6**

3 fennel bulbs, tops and fronds removed (save them for garnish)
1 medium red onion, thinly sliced
Salt and fresh ground black pepper, to taste
2 tablespoons extra virgin olive oil
2 tablespoons salted butter
1 orange

Cut each fennel bulb in half, remove stalks and root ends, and cut into ¼-inch slices. Combine with the sliced onion. Add salt and pepper.

Heat the oil and butter together in a large skillet over a medium heat. Add the fennel and onion, and cook, stirring occasionally, for about 10 minutes or until they're caramelized.

Zest then juice the orange. Add juice to the fennel and onion mixture and stir.

Garnish with fronds and orange zest. Serve immediately.

DOLCI

# Biscotti

Growing up, there was always a batch of biscotti in the pantry. These twice-baked biscotti have now become a very trendy dessert in New York City coffee shops. One of the reasons they are so popular is because you can change them according to your favorite flavor additions, which can include chocolate chips, dried cranberries, pistachios, walnuts, pecans, currants, lemon or orange zest, and more. You can also add extracts, such as almond or lemon. For real decadence, you can dip the ends of your biscotti into your favorite melted (dark or white) chocolate.

**Makes about 3 dozen**

½ cup vegetable or canola oil, or unsalted butter (softened)
¾ cup granulated white sugar
2 teaspoons vanilla extract
2 eggs
1¾ cups all-purpose flour
¼ teaspoon salt
1 teaspoon baking powder
1 cup of your choice of coarsely chopped nuts or dried berries (it can also be a combination)

Preheat the oven to 350°F.

Grease a baking sheet or line with parchment paper.

Mix the oil (or cream the butter) and sugar together in a large bowl. Add the vanilla and the eggs, one at a time, and stir until well blended.

In a separate bowl, combine the flour, salt, and baking powder. Gradually add the dry ingredients to the wet mixture, stirring constantly. Add your nuts or any other addition. Continue mixing until blended. The dough will be slightly sticky, so you should flour your hands as you work with it.

Divide the dough into either 2 logs (12 by 2 inches) or 4 logs (6 by 2 inches). Make sure you place them several inches (at least 3 inches) apart because they will expand.

Bake for 35 minutes or until the logs are light brown. Let cool for 10 minutes.

Then turn the heat down to 275°F. Using a sharp, serrated knife, cut the logs into diagonal slices, about ¾-inch long. You can place them on their sides (or stand them upright on the baking sheet) and bake them for an additional 10 minutes. (This is why they are called twice-baked.) Cool before serving.

BREAKING BREAD ON *Friday*

ANTIPASTI

# Insalata di Mare e Servita nel Radicchio

## (Seafood Salad in a Radicchio Cup)

Festive and easy to make, this appetizer was a big hit with Paul, who loved my creative plating, as did guests. I like to present this salad atop a rich, purple, radicchio leaf–lined martini glass. Perfect for a special luncheon or celebration, served with a leafy salad (and perhaps a nice glass of wine). You can also adjust the ingredients (the seafood should total about 2 pounds) depending on what is available and, as always, what you enjoy most. This, however, is my favorite combination. I always make a little extra.

**Serves 6**

¼ cup extra virgin olive oil
1 clove garlic, minced
2 tablespoons finely chopped fresh Italian flat leaf parsley
¼ teaspoon red chili flakes
1 pound squid tubes and tentacles
½ pound medium shrimp, peeled, de-veined, and tails removed
½ pound bay scallops
1 head radicchio
1 small red onion, peeled and finely sliced, for garnish
Salt and fresh ground black pepper, to taste
2 lemons

To prepare dressing, whisk together juice from one lemon, olive oil, garlic, parsley, and the red chili flakes. Set aside.

Cut the squid into ½-inch thick rings. Cut the tentacles into small pieces. In a large pot of boiling water, cook the scallops, shrimp, and calamari for 2 minutes. Drain and shock with cold water (to stop the cooking). Place the cooked seafood in a large bowl, add salt and pepper. Toss with the dressing, cover, and refrigerate for at least an hour.

Prepare your radicchio cups: Pull away the leaves from the stalk, and place the leaves to blanket the bottom of six martini glasses (or serving plates). Cut the remaining lemon into six segments. Divide the seafood mixture into your prepared cups or plates and top with the sliced red onion, and a slice of lemon. Serve immediately.

PRIMI PIATTI

# Pasta con Salsa di Mascarpone e Zafferano

*(Pasta with a Saffron Mascarpone Sauce)*

Because of L'Aquila's proximity to the Navelli Valley, where precious saffron is harvested, there is a great flavor and color influence in several of their dishes. I have made this saffron-kissed sauce with mascarpone, but don't be afraid to try it with ricotta or soft cheeses that you enjoy. I have also made this with artichokes in place of zucchini or with other pasta shapes. Be creative—and have fun!

**Serves 6**

1 pound *rigatoncini* pasta
2 tablespoons extra virgin olive oil
4 tablespoons salted butter
1 zucchini, very thinly sliced
Salt and fresh ground black pepper, to taste
1 pinch saffron
½ cup mascarpone cheese
½ cup grated fresh mozzarella
½ cup freshly grated Parmigiano cheese

Heat the olive oil in a large skillet over medium-high heat. Add the zucchini and season with salt and pepper. Add the saffron. Cook, stirring frequently, for 3 to 4 minutes. Lower the heat and stir in the mascarpone, fresh mozzarella, and grated cheese.

Using a large pot, cook the pasta according to package instructions until it is al dente. Drain the pasta, but reserve about ¼ cup of the pasta water. Add the mascarpone mixture, along with the remaining butter, and toss to combine. Add the reserved pasta water slowly, as needed, to make the sauce a bit creamier.

Serve immediately.

SECONDI PIATTI

# Dentice al Forno con Salsa di Burro e Limone

### (Baked Red Snapper with a Lemon-Butter Sauce)

Paul always loved this dish, especially on Christmas Eve (though I have to confess that his favorite used to be red snapper's difficult-to-eat cousin, the smaller and more delicate trilia or red mullet, which his family traditionally prepared on that same holiday). Snapper always gets rave reviews in my home. Simple and elegant, this dish is complemented by any vegetable or pasta.

**Serves 6**

3 large snapper fillets (about 2 pounds), with skin
3 tablespoons salted butter
Salt and fresh ground black pepper, to taste
2 teaspoons capers (salted or brine)
2 lemons, sliced
2 tablespoons chopped fresh Italian flat leaf parsley
2 tablespoons salmon roe (optional)

Preheat the oven to 350°F.

Lightly butter a baking dish with 1 tablespoon of the butter.

Pat the fish dry with paper towels, sprinkle both sides with salt and pepper, and place it in the baking dish, skin-side down. The salted capers should be rinsed. Top the fish with the butter, capers, and a layer of lemon slices.

Cover the dish with foil and bake, basting frequently, for about 30 minutes or until the fish flakes easily and is no longer translucent.

Transfer to a serving platter, sprinkle with parsley, add lemon slices and decorate with salmon roe, if desired.

Serve immediately.

CONTORNI

# Fagiolini all'Agro (Green Beans with Lemon)

Green Beans are incredibly versatile, and I enjoy them in many ways. They are as good stewed with tomatoes as they are sautéed with garlic, olive oil, and red chilies. Though I love green beans as a side dish for just about any meal, I also love them in a salad the next day. (I told you—I grew up with that "What's-the-next-meal" mentality!) In this recipe, I have also substituted red wine vinegar (or my dad's homemade vinegar) for the lemon juice.

**Serves 6**

1 pound green beans
2 to 3 tablespoons extra virgin olive oil
Juice from 1 lemon
1 clove garlic, sliced
Salt and fresh ground black pepper, to taste

Trim the green beans.

In a large saucepan over medium-high heat, bring water to a gentle boil then add 2 tablespoons of salt. Add the green beans and cook, uncovered, until crisp-tender, about 5 minutes.

Immediately transfer to an ice bath to retain the green color.

Drain the water and toss with the dressing of olive oil, sliced garlic, and lemon juice. Add a pinch of salt and black pepper to taste.

Serve at room temperature.

CONTORNI

# Fritto Misto di Funghi (Sautéed Mushrooms Medley)

This medley can be orchestrated according to what you like and what's available. Personally, I love porcinis, but I also enjoy combining them with other favorites, such as portabellos and criminis. The earthy, rich taste of mushrooms makes this dish a perfect side for your *secondo* or served with one of your favorite cheeses, such as Parmigiano, blue, mozzarella, or *fontina*, and a crusty loaf of bread. I have used the leftovers to add to the pasta and mushroom recipe on page 76.

**Serves 6**

2 pounds of mushrooms (portabellos, porcinis, and criminis)
2 cloves garlic, chopped
2 tablespoons extra virgin olive oil
2 tablespoons salted butter
Salt and fresh ground black pepper, to taste

Clean the mushrooms, trim the stems, and slice.

In a large skillet, add the butter and olive oil over medium heat. Add the garlic and cook, stirring frequently, until the garlic starts to turn golden brown.

Add the sliced mushrooms and sauté, stirring frequently, for about 10 minutes or until they are lightly browned. Season with salt and pepper.

Serve immediately.

CONTORNI

# Peperoni Arrostiti (Roasted Peppers)

At the end of the summer, when I was a child growing up in Toronto, it seemed like all the people in my neighborhood synchronized their red-pepper roasting! The smell, which brings together beautiful notes of sweetness and barbecue, would waft through the streets. Today I often roast my red peppers right in my country kitchen, in my oven, as in this recipe. The aroma of the peppers while they are roasting brings me back to warm memories. I recommend keeping them on hand to serve as a treat atop some crusty bread with a drizzle of extra virgin olive oil.

**Serves 6**

8 large bell peppers (red and yellow)
3 tablespoons extra virgin olive oil
1 clove garlic, sliced
Salt and fresh ground black pepper, to taste

Preheat the oven to 450°F.

Wash the peppers and pat them dry. Lightly coat the peppers with 1 tablespoon of olive oil. Make sure there is a thin layer of olive oil on all the peppers and place them in a single layer in the pan. Lightly season with salt.

Roast the peppers, turning, until the skins blister and turn black on all sides.

Remove them from the oven and tightly cover the pan with foil, or seal them in a paper bag until they cool. The steam will allow the skins will peel away easily. Remove the skins, tops, and seeds (but don't rinse, or you'll wash away precious oils and flavor). Slice the peppers into 1-inch strips and place them in a bowl. Add the remaining olive oil and sliced garlic.

This dish is perfect at room temperature.

## DOLCI

# Torta di Caffè (Coffee Cake)

Coffee breaks were made for this coffee cake! When it's not the middle of the work day, you can drizzle a bit of liquor on top and serve it with coffee ice cream and dark chocolate shavings. I've also substituted the walnut filling with chopped dried figs and honey or lemon jam with sweet lemon rind. Have fun and be creative with the filling. If it makes it to the freezer, it keeps very well for last-minute guests.

**Serves 6**

¾ cup unsalted butter, plus 2 tablespoons for the filling
3 cups all-purpose flour
¾ teaspoon baking soda
1 tablespoon baking powder
½ teaspoon salt
1½ cup white granulated sugar
½ cup firmly packed brown sugar
1 teaspoon vanilla extract
3 large eggs
1½ cups sour cream
1½ teaspoons cinnamon
½ cup chopped walnuts
Confectioner's sugar and whole walnuts for decorating

Preheat the oven to 350°F.

Lightly grease a Bundt or tube pan with butter. In a bowl, combine the flour, baking soda, baking powder, and salt. Set aside.

Cream ¾ cup of softened butter with 1 cup of the white granulated sugar and brown sugar with an electric hand mixer. Continue stirring until the mixture becomes fluffy. Add in the vanilla. Stir in the eggs, one at a time, add sour cream, and continue mixing until everything is well blended. Add the flour mixture, a little at a time, until it is blended and smooth.

In a small bowl, combine the ingredients for the walnut filling: the walnuts, the remaining (½ cup) white granulated sugar, and the cinnamon. In a small saucepan, melt the remaining 2 tablespoons of butter and add it to the walnut filling.

Pour half of the batter into the greased pan and, using a spatula, even it out. Spread the walnut filling over the batter and then add the rest of the batter over the filling.

Bake in the center of the oven for approximately 1 hour. Test with a toothpick. Let stand at least 10 minutes before removing the cake from the pan. Lightly dust with confectioner's sugar and top with walnuts before serving.

BREAKING BREAD ON *Saturday*

ANTIPASTI

# Panini Imbottiti (Panini Appetizer)

These tasty sandwiches always remind me of my days with Paul in L'Aquila. We would go for an afternoon snack of perfectly toasted paninis—and an ice-cold beer—in one of my favorite outdoor cafés. Paninis are wonderful little teasers to start your meal, or even lunchtime fare with a big leafy salad. You simply can't go wrong with the perfect threesome: prosciutto, fresh creamy mozzarella, and perfectly ripe tomatoes. Here I also suggest pouring some olive oil into a ramekin, perhaps with a sprinkle of red chili flakes for side dipping.

**Serves 6**

12 slices crusty Italian bread, cut ½ inch thick
6 slices excellent-quality thinly sliced prosciutto
6 slices fresh mozzarella
6 slices tomato
3 to 4 tablespoons extra virgin olive oil
Salt

Preheat a grill or pan to medium-high or use a two-sided electric grill.

Place 6 pieces of bread on a cutting board. Top each with a slice of prosciutto, a slice of mozzarella, and a slice of tomato. Then top with another piece of bread.

Lightly brush both sides of the bread with 2 tablespoons of the olive oil. Add a pinch of salt. Grill the bread on each side for several minutes, until it's toasted and crisp.

Serve immediately.

PRIMI PIATTI

# Pasta e Lenticchie (Pasta and Lentils)

Fall in L'Aquila is not unlike fall in New York: the days can be bright and warm, while the nights are brisk and chilly. This dish is perfect for those days when the skies are gray, and you want something to warm you up. If you don't have dried lentils on hand, simply reach for a can from your pantry. (See my pantry supply list on page 134.) I prefer the dry lentils. As another variation, I've also added fresh sausage while the lentils are cooking. This is a dish prepared in the town of Santo Stefano di Sessanio. They are famous in Italy for its production of lentils. Did you know that this town has been referred to as the "Tuscany of Abruzzo"? Fantastic!

**Serves 6**

1½ cups dry lentils (or canned, drained, and rinsed)
2 tablespoons extra virgin olive oil
4 ounces pancetta (cut in ¼-inch pieces)
2 medium onions, chopped
1 clove garlic, finely chopped
1 pound spaghetti (or egg noodles)
Salt and fresh ground black pepper, to taste
Freshly grated Parmigiano cheese
2 tablespoons finely chopped fresh Italian flat leaf parsley

In a medium saucepan, bring salted water to a boil. Add the lentils, cover, and continue cooking over medium heat, stirring occasionally, until tender but not mushy, about 20 minutes. Drain and set aside. (If you are using canned lentils, you can add them directly to the frying pan after you sauté the pancetta.)

Using a large pot, cook the pasta according to the package instructions until it is al dente.

In the meantime, heat olive oil in a medium sauté pan over medium-high heat. Add the pancetta, onions, and garlic. Continue cooking, stirring frequently, until the pancetta is golden, about 7 minutes. Combine with the lentils and season with salt and pepper. Drain the pasta, but reserve ½ cup of pasta water. Toss the lentils and gradually add water until creamy. Sprinkle with Parmigiano and garnish with parsley.

Serve immediately.

PRIMI PIATTI

# Spaghetti Aglio, Olio, e Peperoncino

*(Spaghetti with Garlic, Oil, and Chili Peppers)*

Peperoncino—Italy's chili peppers—are always in my parents' home. When I was growing up, Mom and Nonna put them in everything from sauces to vegetables, meats, and sandwiches. My dad also enjoys them pickled, as part of an antipasto. This super-simple pasta is a standby for me when guests suddenly stop by. Since I don't always have peperoncino on hand, I sometimes use red chili flakes, which never fail to give me the spark I'm looking for. Perhaps I like a bit more of the *picanti* (spiciness) than you. Here, you have the choice of turning the heat up or down (you can always go lower and then give your guests the option of turning it up).

**Serves 6**

1 pound spaghetti
2 tablespoons extra virgin olive oil
3 cloves garlic, minced
Peperoncino thinly sliced or red chili flakes, to taste
3 tablespoons finely chopped fresh Italian flat leaf parsley
¼ cup freshly grated Parmigiano cheese
Salt

Using a large pot, cook the pasta according to the package instructions until it is al dente.

Meanwhile, in a medium-sized sauté pan, heat the oil over medium heat. Add the garlic and cook, stirring frequently. When the garlic is slightly golden, add the sliced peperoncino or red chili flakes and sauté them for a few more minutes. (Keep an eye on the garlic, though, because it becomes bitter if it becomes too dark.)

Drain the pasta and add it to the sauté pan. Toss with the garlic mixture and parsley. Add salt to taste. Sprinkle with Parmigiano.

Serve immediately.

SECONDI PIATTI

# Pollo Arrosto con Aglio e Rosmarino

*(Roasted Chicken with Rosemary and Garlic)*

Few dishes are as comforting as roasted chicken! I especially like this one, because it sends the beautiful aroma of rosemary wafting through my house. Serve with the Oven Roasted Potatoes (page 128), along with Caprese Salad (page 56) or a salad of your choice. And don't forget: if you have any leftover chicken, you can always make a lunch of fabulous paninis!

**Serves 6**

1 chicken (3 to 4 pounds)
3 to 4 tablespoons extra virgin olive oil
3 cloves garlic, minced
3 tablespoons fresh rosemary, chopped
¼ teaspoon fresh ground black pepper
1 tablespoon coarse salt

Preheat the oven to 375°F.

In a small bowl, combine the olive oil, garlic, rosemary, salt, and pepper and mix well. Using a spoon (or your fingers), rub the mixture under the skin and outside the chicken until it's well coated.

Place on a rack in a baking pan and bake until the chicken is golden brown and cooked through, about 1½ hours. Check the chicken periodically and baste several times.

Let the chicken sit for about 10 minutes before carving. Then cut into pieces and serve warm.

CONTORNI

# Cavolfiori al Forno (Baked Cauliflower)

Before I knew about its curative powers, and even before I enjoyed it with Paul in L'Aquila, I loved cauliflower. Rich in vitamin C and antioxidants, this white veggie is especially tasty. (I confess, I love eating it anywhere—but it does taste better to me in Italy!) What I enjoy about cauliflower is that it works well with so many other dishes. You can enjoy it instead of its starchier cousin, the potato, with Roast Chicken (page 110) or any grilled meat or fish. Of course, being the next-day girl that I am, I put any leftovers on top of my next day's salad.

**Serves 6**

1 large cauliflower (4 cups), cut into florets
1 clove garlic, minced
¼ cup bread crumbs (unseasoned)
2 tablespoons finely chopped fresh Italian flat leaf parsley
½ cup freshly grated Parmigiano cheese
3 tablespoons extra virgin olive oil
Salt and fresh ground black pepper, to taste

Preheat the oven to 375°F.

Using a large pot, fill halfway with water and bring to a boil. Add 2 tablespoons of salt and add the florets. Boil for 5 minutes and drain the cauliflower.

In a large bowl, toss the cauliflower with garlic and 2 tablespoons of olive oil. Spread the cauliflower evenly in a shallow baking dish.

In a small bowl, combine the bread crumbs, parsley and grated Parmigiano. Spread this mixture evenly over the cauliflower. Drizzle the remaining olive oil on top. Season with a pinch of salt and pepper.

Bake uncovered for about 8 minutes. Stir the cauliflower and continue baking for another 8 minutes or so (for a total of 15 to 20 minutes), or until golden.

Serve warm.

CONTORNI

# Piselli e Guanciale (Peas and Guanciale)

This perfect-with-just-about-anything side dish is as colorful as it is tasty. If you want to add even more color, try using yellow tomatoes, or those beautiful heirlooms when they're in season. Guanciale is an unsmoked Italian bacon. If you're having trouble finding it, you can use pancetta or excellent-quality bacon. Another nice feature of this side dish? It can double as a pasta topping: *pasta e piselli*!

**Serves 6**

2 to 3 tablespoons extra virgin olive oil
4 ounces finely diced guanciale
2 medium onions, chopped
1 pound peas (fresh or frozen)
2 medium tomatoes, chopped
Salt and fresh ground black pepper, to taste

In a frying pan, heat the olive oil over medium-high heat. Sauté the onions and guanciale, stirring frequently until golden, about 5 minutes.

Stir in the peas and tomatoes and continue cooking for 5 to 7 minutes. Season with salt and pepper (make sure you taste it first) and toss together well.

Serve warm.

DOLCI

# Torta di Noci (Walnut Cake)

This is another classic Italian dessert that's as perfect for after dinner as it is for afternoon espresso—or, I confess, a breakfast treat! I also appreciate it for its flexibility: you can substitute the walnuts with pecans or, if you're not a big candied fruit fan, simply leave them out.

**Serves 6**

1 cup unsalted butter, at room temperature
5 eggs, separated
1 cup white granulated sugar
½ teaspoon salt
1½ teaspoons baking powder
¾ cup all-purpose flour
2 cups finely chopped walnuts or pecans
4 ounces bittersweet chocolate, finely chopped
1 cup candied fruit (optional)
Confectioner's sugar for decoration

Preheat the oven to 350°F.

Grease and flour a 9-inch cake pan.

Using an electric hand mixer, cream the butter with the sugar. Beat in the egg yolks one at a time. In a bowl, combine the baking powder, flour and salt. Add to the egg mixture.

In a separate bowl, beat the egg whites until they are stiff and fold them into the batter. Add the finely chopped chocolate, nuts, and candied fruit and combine well.

Pour the batter into the prepared cake pan, and bake for about 45 minutes, or until a toothpick inserted into the center comes out clean. Wait for about 15 minutes before removing the cake from the pan. Sprinkle with confectioner's sugar. Serve warm or at room temperature.

BREAKING BREAD ON *Sunday*

ANTIPASTI

# Crostini

The salty flavor of the anchovies, combined with the creamy mozzarella, is balanced beautifully with the meat of the tomatoes and the crunch of the Italian bread pieces. This is an ideal afternoon snack—with a glass of wine, of course—or the perfect start to your Sunday (or any day) dinner.

**Serves 6**

12 pieces of Italian bread, cut into ¼-inch thick slices
12 slices of fresh mozzarella (1 pound)
6 anchovy fillets, each sliced in half (you'll need 12 pieces total)
4 medium tomatoes, finely diced
1 tablespoon dried oregano
2 tablespoons extra virgin olive oil
¼ cup salted butter
Salt and fresh ground black pepper, to taste

Preheat the oven to 375°F.

Lightly butter the tops of the bread. Arrange the bread on a single layer on the baking sheet (you may need 2 sheets). Place a slice of mozzarella cheese on each slice of bread. Follow that with a slice of anchovy and a spoonful of tomatoes. Sprinkle with oregano, salt, pepper, and a drizzle of olive oil on top.

Bake in the oven for approximately 7 to 8 minutes, or until the mozzarella cheese is melted.

Serve immediately.

PRIMI PIATTI

# Pasta alla Chitarra con Polpettine di Paolo

*(Pasta alla Chitarra with Paul's Meatballs)*

Paul's meatballs were famous—not only for their flavor, but also for their size: he liked them small! Though, he was a fabulous cook, once he let me in the kitchen (and taught me how to make his favorites), he didn't come back in. As queen of the kitchen, I began making his favorites, like this one. We would sometimes serve these meatballs on top of *pasta alla chitarra*, Abruzzo's famous pasta. This is made with a pasta guitar (it looks like a harp) to produce squarish-shaped spaghetti. You can also use spaghetti or your favorite pasta. Growing up, my mother would serve it with our favorite *rigatoni* or *penne* pasta.

**Serves 6**

- 3 cups of tomato sauce (see page 44)
- 1 pound ground pork
- 1 pound ground beef
- 2 eggs
- 1½ cup freshly grated Parmigiano cheese
- 1 tablespoon fresh Italian flat leaf parsley, chopped
- 1 cup bread crumbs (unseasoned)
- 1 clove garlic, minced
- ½ teaspoon fresh ground black pepper
- 2 teaspoons salt
- 1 pound of pasta alla chitarra (fresh)
- 3 tablespoons extra virgin olive oil

In a large bowl, combine the pork, beef, eggs, bread crumbs and 1 cup of cheese. Add the parsley, garlic, salt and pepper and combine well. Using your hands, form quarter-sized meatballs and place them on a tray. (If the mixture is too stick, rinse your hands under cold water and leave them slightly damp.)

Heat the oil in a frying pan over medium heat. Fry the meatballs in batches, turning them frequently, until they form a nice brown crispy layer on the outside and are cooked through (approximately 10 to 12 minutes). Drain them on paper towels.

Heat the tomato sauce in a medium-sized pot over medium heat. Add the meatballs and cook on low heat for 30 minutes.

Using a large pot, cook the pasta according to the package instructions until it is al dente. Drain the pasta and return it to the pot. Add the sauce with meatballs and toss well. Top with remaining Parmigiano and serve.

PRIMI PIATTI

# Le Lasagne di Paolo (Paul's Lasagna)

One of the dishes that Paul taught me to make, and then requested often, was his famous lasagna. Though he sometimes asked that it be made with his meatballs (see page 122), here I have cheated, to make it a bit quicker, making it with a Bolognese sauce. (When you've got the time, I insist you make the meatballs with it.) This lasagna is, as Paul promised it would be from day one, a work of art. I like to use fresh noodles, but, believe me, this works well with packaged, too! I like to garnish my lasagne with my "basil top hats": fresh basil with sun-dried tomatoes.

**Serves 6**

4 tablespoons extra virgin olive oil
1 pound lasagna noodles
1 medium onion, finely chopped
1 clove garlic, finely chopped
1 small carrot, coarsely chopped
1 pound ground pork
1 pound ground beef
1 tablespoon salt
½ teaspoon fresh ground black pepper
3 tablespoons chopped fresh basil leaves
2 cans chopped plum tomatoes (28 ounces each)
1 can tomato paste (5 ounces)
1 cup water
6 hard-boiled eggs, coarsely chopped
2 cups shredded mozzarella cheese
1 cup freshly grated Parmigiano cheese

Bolognese sauce: Pour 3 tablespoons of olive oil into a large pot over medium heat. Sauté the onion, garlic, and carrot, about 3 minutes. Add the ground pork and beef, and cook, stirring occasionally, for about 5 minutes or until evenly browned. Add salt, pepper, basil, tomatoes, tomato paste, and water. Simmer over medium-low heat for 20 minutes.

Preheat the oven to 350°F. Lightly grease a baking pan with olive oil for the noodles.

Using a large pot, cook the pasta according to the package instructions until it is al dente. Drain the noodles and then place them on a prepared greased sheet pan until you are ready to assemble the lasagna.

Layer a 9-by-13-inch baking pan with about a ¼ cup of the Bolognese sauce. Arrange enough noodles lengthwise over the sauce to form a single layer. Top with a layer of Bolognese sauce, chopped egg, mozzarella, and cheese. Repeat for 4 to 5 layers, or until you've used all the noodles and other ingredients. Sprinkle the lasagna with Parmigiano and mozzarella on top. Cover the lasagna with aluminium foil and bake it for 25 minutes. Remove the foil and bake for 10 minutes, or until totally cooked through and nicely browned on the top. Remove the lasagna from the oven and let it set for 15 minutes before serving.

SECONDI PIATTI

# Cosciotto d'Agnello Arrosto (Roast Leg of Lamb)

Lamb always reminds me of a special holiday, which makes it perfect for Sunday dinner. The smell of the garlic and the rosemary cooking is so warm and welcoming. Despite the higher price tag, I prefer cooking spring lambs; the younger ones have less of a gamey aroma. (Trust your butcher to help you with this.) Serve your roast lamb with Oven-Roasted Potatoes (page 128) and a green leafy salad.

**Serves 6**

1 leg of lamb, bone in or boneless (3 to 4 pounds)
⅓ cup extra virgin olive oil
5 sprigs of rosemary, remove the leaves from stem (chopped)
2 tablespoons coarse salt
1 tablespoon fresh ground black pepper
4 cloves garlic, 3 minced, 1 sliced
2 cups dry white wine

Preheat the oven to 400°F.

Wash and pat the lamb dry. Place the lamb in a roasting pan.

In a small bowl, combine the olive oil, rosemary, salt, and pepper. Using your fingers, rub this rosemary-oil paste all over the leg of lamb. Then, using a sharp knife, poke little holes into the meat and insert pieces of garlic. Top the meat with the white wine. Add 1 cup of water to the pan.

Place the lamb in the oven and roast it for 30 minutes. Then reduce the oven temperature to 350°F and continue to cook for about 1 hour, basting occasionally, until the meat thermometer registers between 145° and 150°F (for medium-rare).

Remove the lamb from the pan and rest it on a cutting board for 15 minutes before carving.

CONTORNI

# Patate Arrostite (Oven-Roasted Potatoes)

If you're a starch lover like me, you'll enjoy these with all of your favorite meat or chicken dishes. It's one vegetable that I never get tired of and is always welcomed by my guests. Who would have thought with just potatoes! If any make it to the next day, I add the leftovers to a frittata for breakfast or anytime.

**Serves 6**

2 pounds Yukon gold potatoes (approximately 6 medium)
3 tablespoons extra virgin olive oil
6 cloves garlic, halved
Leaves from 2 sprigs rosemary (or to taste), coarsely chopped
Salt and fresh ground black pepper, to taste

Preheat the oven to 375°F.

Peel the potatoes and cut them into cubes about 1 inch in size. In a roasting pan, toss the potatoes with oil, salt, pepper, garlic, and rosemary.

Place the pan in the oven and bake for about 45 minutes. Stir the potatoes occasionally until they are evenly cooked (lightly crisp on the outside, soft but not mushy on the inside).

Serve warm.

CONTORNI

# Insalata di Rucola e Radicchio

## (Arugula and Radicchio Salad)

*I* love the fantastic bittersweet flavor of this salad, which is equally pleasing to the eye as it is to the palette. A splash of truffle oil is heavenly here! You can easily make this into a complete meal by serving it alongside some sausage. It's great the next day, too, on top of a Panini. It's perfect with the recipe on page 104.

**Serves 6**

2 heads of radicchio
2 bunches baby arugula
½ cup walnuts (or sliced almonds, pine nuts, hazelnuts)
Salt and fresh ground black pepper, to taste
3 tablespoons extra virgin olive oil
1 tablespoon balsamic vinegar
Shavings or chunks of pecorino cheese (or goat cheese)

Cut the radicchio in half and then into ¼-inch strips. Trim off any roots or stems from the baby arugula, wash the leaves thoroughly, and pat dry

Place the radicchio in a large bowl with the arugula. Add the chopped walnuts, salt, and pepper. In a small bowl, whisk together the olive oil and balsamic vinegar and pour on top of the greens. Toss well.

Add the shavings of pecorino and serve.

DOLCI

# Pizzelle

Italian waffle cookies, or pizzelle (which literally means small pizzas), are quite popular in the Abruzzo region of Italy. If you don't have a pizzelle maker, I highly recommend investing in one. Believe me, it's worth it just to make these tasty treats. Pizzelle were always Paul's favorite dessert; he loved them so much that I'd often make batches to keep in the freezer so that I could pull them out upon request. What I like about pizzelle, aside from their taste, is their flexibility: you can add cocoa with the sugar and make a chocolate version, or spread some hazelnut cream on one and top with another. Plain and simple pizzelle with ice cream are also dreamy…

**Makes about 36 pizzelle**

1¾ cup all purpose flour
2 teaspoons baking powder
¾ cup white granulated sugar
1 teaspoon salt
½ cup unsalted butter
3 large eggs
2 tablespoons anise (or other extract)

Pre-heat the pizzelle maker.

In a bowl, combine the flour, baking powder, and salt. Set aside. In another bowl, combine the butter and sugar and mix until smooth. Add anise and then the eggs, one at a time, until well blended. Pour in the dry ingredients and mix well.

Lightly spray the pizzelle maker with vegetable oil (unless you have a non-stick version).

Drop the batter by the tablespoon onto the pizzelle iron, and cook, gauging the timing (usually less than a minute) according to the manufacturer's instructions or until golden.

Serve with your favorite toppings.

# Pantry Page

*O*f course my first choice for any ingredients is always fresh, but let's face it: sometimes we just don't have the time! Just like my mother—and her mother—always said, it's essential to have emergency items in your pantry. A well-stocked pantry will help you in times of unexpected company, or when you're in a rush to create a meal but you don't have the time to do any extra shopping. Here, I offer you my master list of must-have items.

Anchovies

Artichokes

Baking powder

Baking soda

Black olives

Black pepper (I prefer whole peppercorns to grind fresh as needed)

Capers

Chocolate (dark and white)

Coffee: espresso beans

Container of bread crumbs

Container of broth or bouillon cubes

Dried fruit: raisins, apricots, cranberries, prunes

Dried herbs: bay leaves, oregano, thyme, rosemary, red chili flakes, or your favorite

Dried beans: lentils (green or brown), red kidney, or your favorite

Dry pasta: spaghetti, linguini, pastina, or your favorite

Dry porcini mushrooms

Flour

Garlic

Mustard

Nuts: pine, walnut, almonds

Olive oil (extra virgin)

Plum tomatoes

Rice: basmati, Arborio

Roasted peppers

Salt: kosher, table, and sea salt

Spelt or barley

Sugar: granulated white, confectioner's (in Canada, it is more commonly known as icing sugar), and brown sugar

Tomato paste

Tuna (packed in oil)

Vanilla extract

Vinegar: red wine, balsamic

# Measurement Conversions

Since I'm Canadian *and* American, I thought it would be best to show both types of measurements on this page. For those of us who were brought up with other measuring tools, such as glasses, mugs, espresso cups, or regular utensils (I know some of you will relate!), this standardizes it a bit. Of course you should feel free to vary the measurements with most of my dishes—except for the desserts, which require more exact amounts.

| U.S. Standard | Metric |
| --- | --- |
| ¼ teaspoon | 1 ml |
| ½ teaspoon | 2 ml |
| 1 teaspoon | 5 ml |
| 1 tablespoon | 15 ml |
| ¼ cup | 60 ml |
| ½ cup | 120 ml |
| 1 cup | 240 ml |
| 1 oz. | 28 g |
| ¼ lb. | 113 g |
| ½ lb. | 230 g |
| 1 lb. | 450 g |

# Index

Almond
    Amaretti Cookies/Biscotti Amaretti 36
Anchovies
    Crostini 120
    Romaine Lettuce Salad with Shaved Parmigiano Cheese/Insalata con Scaglie di Parmigiano 32
Antipasti, Recipe for,
    Bruschetta 24
    Caprese Salad/Insalata Caprese 56
    Crostini 120
    Grilled Eggplant with Cured Black Olives and Basil/Melanzane alla Griglia con Olive e Basilico 72
    Panini Appetizer/Panini Imbottiti 104
    Prosciutto with Melon/Prosciutto e Melone 40
    Seafood Salad in a Radicchio Cup/Insalata di Mare e Servita nel Radicchio 88
Apple
    Apple Cake/Torta di Mele 68
Artichokes
    Baked Artichokes/Carciofi al Forno 64
Arugula
    Arugula and Radicchio Salad/Insalata di Rucola e Radicchio 130
Baccalà
    Baked Salt Cod/Baccalà al Forno 46
Bacon
    Spelt Soup/Minestra di Farro 42
Beans
    Pasta and Beans/Pasta e Fagioli 26
Beef
    Pasta alla Chitarra with Paul's Meatballs/Pasta alla Chitarra con Polpettine di Paolo 122
    Paul's Lasagna/Le Lasagne di Paolo 124

Bell Peppers
    Roasted Peppers/Peperoni Arrostiti 98
    Roasted Stuffed Peppers with Sausage/Peperoni Arrostiti Ripieni con Salsiccia 48
Bread/Bread Crumbs
    Baked Artichokes/Carciofi al Forno 64
    Baked Cauliflower/Cavolfiori al Forno 112
    Baked Pasta with Tomatoes and Capers/Pasta al Forno con Pomodori e Capperi 60
    Bruschetta 24
    Crostini 120
    Panini Appetizer/Panini Imbottiti 104
    Pasta alla Chitarra with Paul's Meatballs/Pasta alla Chitarra con Polpettine di Paolo 122
    Roasted Stuffed Peppers with Sausage/Peperoni Arrostiti Ripieni con Salsiccia 48
    Veal Cutlets/Cotolette di Vitello 30
Broccoli Rabe
    Broccoli Rabe/Rapini 50
Cantaloupe
    Prosciutto with Melon/Prosciutto e Melone 40
Capers
    Baked Pasta with Tomatoes and Capers/Pasta al Forno con Pomodori e Capperi 60
    Baked Red Snapper with a Lemon-Butter Sauce/Dentice al Forno con Salsa di Burro e Limone 92
    Baked Salt Cod/Baccalà al Forno 46
Carrots
    Paul's Lasagna/Le Lasagne di Paolo 124
    Spaghetti with Tomato Sauce/Spaghetti al Pomodoro 44
    Vegetable Soup with Rice/Minestra di Verdure con Riso 58

Cauliflower
    Baked Cauliflower/Cavolfiori al Forno 112
Celery
    Vegetable Soup with Rice/Minestra di Verdure con Riso 58
Chicken
    Roasted Chicken with Rosemary and Garlic/Pollo Arrosto con Aglio e Rosmarino 110
Contorni, Recipe for,
    Arugula and Radicchio Salad/Insalata di Rucola e Radicchio 130
    Baked Artichokes/Carciofi al Forno 64
    Baked Cauliflower/Cavolfiori al Forno 112
    Boiled Potatoes with Fresh Parsley/Patate Lesse con Prezzemolo Fresco 66
    Broccoli Rabe/Rapini 50
    Caramelized Fennel and Onions with Orange Rind/Finocchio e Cipolla Caramellizate con Scorza d'Arancia 82
    Green Beans with Lemon/Fagiolini all'Agro 94
    Oven-Roasted Potatoes/Patate Arrostite 128
    Peas and Guanciale/Piselli e Guanciale 114
    Roasted Peppers/Peperoni Arrostiti 98
    Romaine Lettuce Salad with Shaved Parmigiano Cheese/Insalata con Scaglie di Parmigiano 32
    Rustic Vegetables with Balsamic Reduction/Verdure Rustiche con Riduzione di Aceto Balsamico 34
    Sautéed Mushrooms Medley/Fritto Misto di Funghi 96
Dolci, Recipe for,
    Amaretti Cookies/Biscotti Amaretti 36
    Apple Cake/Torta di Mele 68
    Biscotti 84
    Coffee Cake/Torta di Caffè 100
    Pizzelle 132
    Rustic Apricot Fruit Tart/Crostata d'Albicocca 52
    Walnut Cake/Torta di Noci 116
Eggplant
    Grilled Eggplant with Cured Black Olives and Basil/Melanzane alla Griglia con Olive e Basilico 72
Endive
    Rustic Vegetables with Balsamic Reduction/Verdure Rustiche con Riduzione di Aceto Balsamico 34
Fava Beans
    Vegetable Soup with Rice/Minestra di Verdure con Riso 58
Fennel
    Caramelized Fennel and Onions with Orange Rind/Finocchio e Cipolla Caramellizate con Scorza d'Arancia 82
Green Beans
    Green Beans with Lemon/Fagiolini all'Agro 94
Guanciale
    Peas and Guanciale/Piselli e Guanciale 114
Lamb
    Grilled Lamb Chops/Costolette d'Agnello alla Griglia 62
    Roast Leg of Lamb/Cosciotto d'Agnello Arrosto 126
Lentils
    Pasta and Lentils/Pasta e Lenticchie 106
Mascarpone
    Pasta with a Saffron Mascarpone Sauce/Pasta con Salsa di Mascarpone e Zafferano 90
Mozzarella
    Caprese Salad/Insalata Caprese 56
    Crostini 120
    Panini Appetizer/Panini Imbottiti 104
    Pasta with a Saffron Mascarpone Sauce/Pasta con Salsa di Mascarpone e Zafferano 90
    Paul's Lasagna/Le Lasagne di Paolo 124
Mushroom
    Pasta with Mushrooms/Pasta con Funghi 76
    Sautéed Mushrooms Medley/Fritto Misto di Funghi 96
Olives
    Grilled Eggplant with Cured Black Olives and Basil/Melanzane alla Griglia con Olive e Basilico 72

Onions
- Caramelized Fennel and Onions with Orange Rind/Finocchio e Cipolla Caramellizate con Scorza d'Arancia 82
- Baked Salt Cod/Baccalà al Forno 46
- Pasta and Lentils/Pasta e Lenticchie 106
- Pasta with a Pork Tomato Sauce/Pasta con Salsa di Maiale 28
- Paul's Lasagna/Le Lasagne di Paolo 124
- Roasted Stuffed Peppers with Sausage/Peperoni Arrostiti Ripieni con Salsiccia 48
- Seafood Salad in a Radicchio Cup/Insalata di Mare e Servita nel Radicchio 88
- Spaghetti with Tomato Sauce/Spaghetti al Pomodoro 44
- Spelt Soup/Minestra di Farro 42

Orange/Orange Juice
- Caramelized Fennel and Onions with Orange Rind/Finocchio e Cipolla Caramellizate con Scorza d'Arancia 82
- Orange Glazed Pork/Maiale all'Arancia 78

Pancetta
- Pasta and Lentils/Pasta e Lenticchie 106
- Spelt Soup/Minestra di Farro 42

Parmigiano
- Baked Artichokes/Carciofi al Forno 64
- Baked Cauliflower/Cavolfiori al Forno 112
- Baked Pasta with Tomatoes and Capers/Pasta al Forno con Pomodori e Capperi 60
- Pasta alla Chitarra with Paul's Meatballs/Pasta all Chitarra con Polpettine di Paolo 122
- Pasta and Lentils/Pasta e Lenticchie 106
- Pasta with Mushrooms/Pasta con Funghi 76
- Paul's Lasagna/Le Lasagne di Paolo 124
- Roasted Stuffed Peppers with Sausage/Peperoni Arrostiti Ripieni con Salsiccia 48
- Romaine Lettuce Salad with Shaved Parmigiano Cheese/Insalata con Scaglie di Parmigiano 32
- Spaghetti with Garlic, Oil, and Chili Peppers/Spaghetti Aglio, Olio, e Peperoncino 108

Parmigiano (*continued*)
- Spaghetti with Tomato Sauce/Spaghetti al Pomodoro 44
- Vegetable Soup with Rice/Minestra di Verdure con Riso 58

Pasta
- Baked Pasta with Tomatoes and Capers/Pasta al Forno con Pomodori e Capperi 60
- Gnocchi with Tomato Sauce/Gnocchi al Sugo di Pomodoro 74
- Pasta alla Chitarra with Paul's Meatballs/Pasta all Chitarra con Polpettine di Paolo 122
- Pasta and Beans/Pasta e Fagioli 26
- Pasta and Lentils/Pasta e Lenticchie 106
- Pasta with a Pork Tomato Sauce/Pasta con Salsa di Maiale 28
- Pasta with a Saffron Mascarpone Sauce/Pasta con Salsa di Mascarpone e Zafferano 90
- Pasta with Mushrooms/Pasta con Funghi 76
- Paul's Lasagna/Le Lasagne di Paolo 124
- Spaghetti with Garlic, Oil, and Chili Peppers/Spaghetti Aglio, Olio, e Peperoncino 108
- Spaghetti with Tomato Sauce/Spaghetti al Pomodoro 44

Peas
- Peas and Guanciale/Piselli e Guanciale 114
- Vegetable Soup with Rice/Minestra di Verdure con Riso 58

Pecorino
- Arugula and Radicchio Salad/Insalata di Rucola e Radicchio 130
- Gnocchi with Tomato Sauce/Gnocchi al Sugo di Pomodoro 74
- Pasta with a Pork Tomato Sauce/Pasta con Salsa di Maiale 28
- Spelt Soup/Minestra di Farro 42

Pork. *See also* Bacon, Pancetta, Prosciutto, Sausage
- Orange Glazed Pork/Maiale all'Arancia 78
- Pasta alla Chitarra with Paul's Meatballs/Pasta all Chitarra con Polpettine di Paolo 122
- Pasta with a Pork Tomato Sauce/Pasta con Salsa di Maiale 28
- Paul's Lasagna/Le Lasagne di Paolo 124

Potatoes
- Boiled Potatoes with Fresh Parsley/Patate Lesse con Prezzemolo Fresco 66
- Gnocchi with Tomato Sauce/Gnocchi al Sugo di Pomodoro 74

Potatoes (*continued*)
- Oven-Roasted Potatoes/Patate Arrostite 128
- Rustic Vegetables with Balsamic Reduction/Verdure Rustiche con Riduzione di Aceto Balsamico 34

Primi Piatti, Recipe for,
- Baked Pasta with Tomatoes and Capers/Pasta al Forno con Pomodori e Capperi 60
- Gnocchi with Tomato Sauce/Gnocchi al Sugo di Pomodoro 74
- Pasta alla Chitarra with Paul's Meatballs/Pasta all Chitarra con Polpettine di Paolo 122
- Pasta and Beans/Pasta e Fagioli 26
- Pasta and Lentils/Pasta e Lenticchie 106
- Pasta with Mushrooms/Pasta con Funghi 76
- Pasta with a Pork Tomato Sauce/Pasta con Salsa di Maiale 28
- Pasta with a Saffron Mascarpone Sauce/Pasta con Salsa di Mascarpone e Zafferano 90
- Paul's Lasagna/Le Lasagne di Paolo 124
- Spaghetti with Garlic, Oil, and Chili Peppers/Spaghetti Aglio, Olio, e Peperoncino 108
- Spaghetti with Tomato Sauce/Spaghetti al Pomodoro 44
- Spelt Soup/Minestra di Farro 42
- Vegetable Soup with Rice/Minestra di Verdure con Riso 58

Prosciutto
- Panini Appetizer/Panini Imbottiti 104
- Prosciutto with Melon/Prosciutto e Melone 40

Radicchio
- Arugula and Radicchio Salad/Insalata di Rucola e Radicchio 130
- Seafood Salad in a Radicchio Cup/Insalata di Mare e Servita nel Radicchio 88

Rice
- Vegetable Soup with Rice/Minestra di Verdure con Riso 58

Romaine Lettuce
- Romaine Lettuce Salad with Shaved Parmigiano Cheese/Insalata con Scaglie di Parmigiano 32

Sausage
- Roasted Stuffed Peppers with Sausage/Peperoni Arrostiti Ripieni con Salsiccia 48

Scallops
- Seafood Salad in a Radicchio Cup/Insalata di Mare e Servita nel Radicchio 88

Secondi Piatti, Recipe for,
- Baked Red Snapper with a Lemon-Butter Sauce/Dentice al Forno con Salsa di Burro e Limone 92
- Grilled Lamb Chops/Costolette d'Agnello alla Griglia 62
- Baked Salt Cod/Baccalà al Forno 46
- Orange Glazed Pork/Maiale all'Arancia 78
- Roast Leg of Lamb/Cosciotto d'Agnello Arrosto 126
- Roasted Chicken with Rosemary and Garlic/Pollo Arrosto con Aglio e Rosmarino 110
- Roasted Stuffed Peppers with Sausage/Peperoni Arrostiti Ripieni con Salsiccia 48
- Veal Cutlets/Cotolette di Vitello 30
- Veal Scaloppine in White Wine/Scaloppine al Vino Bianco 80

Shrimp
- Seafood Salad in a Radicchio Cup/Insalata di Mare e Servita nel Radicchio 88

Snapper
- Baked Red Snapper with a Lemon-Butter Sauce/Dentice al Forno con Salsa di Burro e Limone 92

Soup
- Spelt Soup/Minestra di Farro 42
- Vegetable Soup with Rice/Minestra di Verdure con Riso 58

Spelt
- Spelt Soup/Minestra di Farro 42

Squid
- Seafood Salad in a Radicchio Cup/Insalata di Mare e Servita nel Radicchio 88

Swiss Chard
- Vegetable Soup with Rice/Minestra di Verdure con Riso 58

Tomatoes
- Baked Pasta with Tomatoes and Capers/Pasta al Forno con Pomodori e Capperi 60
- Bruschetta 24

Tomatoes (*continued*)
- Caprese Salad/Insalata Caprese 56
- Crostini 120
- Baked Salt Cod/Baccalà al Forno 46
- Panini Appetizer/Panini Imbottiti 104
- Pasta with a Pork Tomato Sauce/Pasta con Salsa di Maiale 28
- Paul's Lasagna/Le Lasagne di Paolo 124
- Peas and Guanciale/Piselli e Guanciale 114
- Romaine Lettuce Salad with Shaved Parmigiano Cheese/Insalata con Scaglie di Parmigiano 32
- Rustic Vegetables with Balsamic Reduction/Verdure Rustiche con Riduzione di Aceto Balsamico 34
- Spaghetti with Tomato Sauce/Spaghetti al Pomodoro 44
- Spelt Soup/Minestra di Farro 42
- Tomato Sauce 44
- Vegetable Soup with Rice/Minestra di Verdure con Riso 58

Veal
- Veal Cutlets/Cotolette di Vitello 30
- Veal Scaloppine in White Wine/Scaloppine al Vino Bianco 80

Walnut
- Arugula and Radicchio Salad/Insalata di Rucola e Radicchio 130
- Biscotti 84
- Coffee Cake/Torta di Caffè 100
- Walnut Cake/Torta di Noci 116

Zucchini
- Pasta with a Saffron Mascarpone Sauce/Pasta con Salsa di Mascarpone e Zafferano 90
- Rustic Vegetables with Balsamic Reduction/Verdure Rustiche con Riduzione di Aceto Balsamico 34